BEETHOVEN VARIATIONS

Ruth Padel

BEETHOVEN VARIATIONS

Poems on a Life

Chatto & Windus

LONDON

1 3 5 7 9 10 8 6 4 2

Chatto & Windus, an imprint of Vintage,
20 Vauxhall Bridge Road,
London SW1V 2SA

Chatto & Windus is part of the Penguin Random House group
of companies whose addresses can be found at
global.penguinrandomhouse.com.

First published by Chatto & Windus in 2020

penguin.co.uk/vintage

A CIP catalogue record for this book is available from
the British Library

ISBN 9781784742515

Autograph manuscript, Opus 131 (v) reproduced courtesy of
Staatsbibliothek zu Berlin PK: http://resolver.staatsbibliothek-berlin.de/
SBB0000DEE600000000
Beethoven silhoutte, c.1786 (3); portrait, c. 1803 (23); portrait, c. 1804:
Granger Historical Picture Archive/Alamy Stock Photo. Beethoven portrait,
c. 1823 (65): Pictorial Press Ltd/Alamy Stock Photo

Typeset in 11/14 pt Fairfield LH
by Integra Software Services Pvt. Ltd, Pondicherry

Printed and bound in Great Britain by Clays Ltd, Elcograf S.p.A.

Penguin Random House is committed to a sustainable future for
our business, our readers and our planet. This book is made from
Forest Stewardship Council® certified paper.

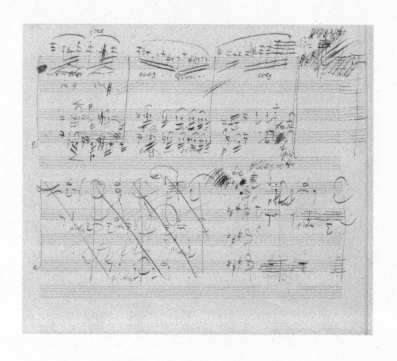

Page from autograph manuscript of
Beethoven's String Quartet in C sharp minor, Opus 131

For the Endellion String Quartet
Andrew Watkinson, Ralph de Souza, Garfield Jackson
and my kind friend David Waterman
with thanks and love

The true artist is not proud. He unfortunately sees that art has no limits; he feels darkly how far he is from the goal; and though he may be admired by others, he is sad not to have reached that point to which his better genius only appears as a distant, guiding sun.

Beethoven, letter to a young pianist, 17 July 1812

I found a music notebook full of musical notes written in fits and starts, additional staves drawn right across the margins. He said, 'I always have a notebook with me. When an idea comes, I put it down at once, I even get up in the middle of the night, otherwise I might forget it.'

Gerhard von Breuning, *Memories of Beethoven*

If you want to think about order, or disruption of order, you have to know what that order was in the first place. Beethoven is a wonderful example. He never does what you think he's going to do, the surprise is perpetual. You know the shape of the music and you think, how is he going to get out of that without a cliché? Then he does something brilliant. That's his genius.

Harrison Birtwhistle, composer

CONTENTS

Music in the Dark of the Mind

Virtuoso

Hero

You Must Not Be Human

LISTEN

Kindest regards to your wife; unfortunately I have none; I found only one who will probably never be mine.

Beethoven to Ferdinand Ries, 8 May 1816

They say the ear bone, shaped like the bowl
of a tiny spoon, lasts longest when we die.
The soul might be like this: hard, necessary,
almost nothing. My parents
got together at a music camp
in farmland of chalk hills. A clarinettist
dropped out of the orchestra, and my dad
queued for the village pay phone,
called a girl he'd just met, hired a tandem bike
and fetched her from the station.

I like to picture her on the edge of knowing,
legs whizzing round, her clarinet case
tied behind. He'd have done that for her,
he always took great pains with making safe.
Between hedgerows of early summer
she's cycling into a lifetime with him.
Look, there we are waiting
for her, five future string-players
hiding among the vetch and willowherb.

She played the piano too. At first
she accompanied him in duets. I can see them
working on Beethoven's Cello Sonata Opus 69.

She's listening to him, he's listening to her.
Questions, answers, the all-you-can't-say
stream to and fro. Angry, agonised, and tender
as the history of marriage. Then we arrived
and she didn't have time to play. It gave me a notion
women do their music-making away from home.

Later she joined an orchestra. I remember her
practising trills from the *Pastoral Symphony*
where a clarinet alone
has to drop perfect sound into perfect silence,
suspend the world, then descend
to the waiting ear. The almost-nothing bone,
that little house of hearing
which brought the two of them together
and which Beethoven lost. So hard to discover
and make perfect, even half-perfect, in yourself.

MUSIC IN THE DARK
OF THE MIND

A tiny boy, standing on a footstool in front of the clavier to which the implacable severities of his father had so early condemned him … Little Louis van Beethoven, in front of the clavier, weeping.

Alexander Wheelock Thayer, *Life of Ludwig van Beethoven*

BIRTHPLACE

Out of nowhere
a stranger appears in the clearing

a now-roped-off chamber
raked ceiling, bare floor

a mother delivered of two babies already

both dead, the last
after only six days

this is how longings arrive

in the world of the given
a gift that changes the balance

echoes of paradise
passion-fruit growing in the dark

the whole branch
dipping from the weight

then springing back

genetic chance
burning on the wick

thrusting to be born.

IDEALISING THE UNATTAINABLE CAN BEGIN VERY EARLY

Little Louis clung with great affection to his grandfather. Though he lost him so soon, he retained the most vivid impression of him.

Dr Franz Wegeler, *Biographical Notes*

It's not the face that stays most truly naked
through a life. What jumps out from this court portrait
of your Flemish grandfather, whose name you bear –
the painting you will lash to a wagon every time you move
along with your manuscripts, piano, single bed
and writing-desk, all rumbling uncovered through city air
furred with floating particles of horse-dung –

is this V of bare chest, the open shirt

within the formal robes, the one soft patch of skin
where he might have cradled you. In all the debris
everywhere you live, jugs of red wine
always on the go, the fevers, smells and flies,
broken love-hopes, slamming doors,
you will find your heart shored up
by meeting the trapped brilliance of his eyes.

IF YOUR FATHER DAMAGED YOU

… the way meteorites
spin in, clustering on Antarctic ice
bare shields of glacier burnished by ferocious wind

because your father is magnetite
dragging all the iron in your soul
into his own force field:

you seal yourself in.
You need nothing but music.
Your answer to obstruction will be fire.

In the little hall
of the house where you were born
the one original surface
is darksilver flagstones
where you might have crawled.
Light falls in shallow hollows
of deciduous rubbed stone
clogged with spume of cleaning fluid
where I imagine your mother
carrying the shopping
your father staggering home drunk
up these stairs – their new-cut wood
now polished to the amber shine of a harvest moon –
to wake you in the middle of the night
stand you for hours on a bench

so you can reach the keys. You cry
as you play, slapped if you make a mistake.
In daylight, he hears you improvise.
Splashing around, he calls it, on a violin.
What rubbish are you scratching now?
Isn't that beautiful? *No!*
You made it up. You're not to do that.
Stop! Or I'll box your ears.

If your father damaged you
the way fierce winds scour glacier ice
where meteorites have fallen from heaven

but he was the one who made you,
beat the notes into you on the clavier
viola, violin

your response to challenge ever after will be attack.
You will need no one. Only the relationship
of sound and key. You improvise.

HIS MOTHER WARMS HIS FEET ON A BOAT

What is marriage but a little joy and then a chain of sorrows?

Maria van Beethoven to Cäcilia Fischer

He goes to school dirty. They say his mother must be dead
call him *Spaniard* because he is dark
tease him about his name. He leaves school

to play the viola
in the briary tangle of an orchestra.
He wears a sea-green coat, a wig, a little sword.

At home he writes concertos
pitching the wonders of modulation
against his father's blows.

Gliding north with her down the Rhine
on a winter concert tour, their one journey together,
she keeps him warm, holding his feet in her lap.

HOME TOWN

In the attic were two telescopes ... That was Beethoven's delight, for the Beethovens loved the Rhine.

Gottfried Fischer, *Memories of Beethoven*

Wherever you look in this town are painted casts
of the famous statue. One at my door
like a street performer,
silver mantle, silver eyes and skin.

In the Town Hall Information Zone
he is lapis lazuli. Face the colour of clear sky
after sunset, body scrawled with white crotchets,
a blizzard of musical snow.

At the end of a street he used to race up laughing,
leading the pack, I see the Rhine
flickering like departure. Chestnut trees
in a skirt of fallen leaves, and six immigrants asleep

in an arcade. Where the house once stood
are rows of little Beethovens, stamped on marzipan.
I see a small boy dashing through these alleys
to play for early mass. Then sullen, dragging his feet

towards some grand door, to teach
a rich child piano. His brothers are useless,

the new babies die. Father drinks his salary.
Mother has a temper. Dry bread and fury

snap through the kitchen. A boy in his bedroom,
seed in the ground. He's strong but he's little.
The heavy viola
bangs his knees as he runs.

ON NOT NEEDING OTHER PEOPLE

Asked why he was rude, he said, 'O excuse me, I was occupied with such a lovely, deep thought I couldn't bear to be disturbed.'

Gottfried Fischer, *Memories of Beethoven*

What is that sound you hear when everything is quiet?
The sun moves through its signs in a minor key
and by the time he's seven he's perfected some holy zone
of concentration, where he's unreachable,
where three descending semitones
say there is answer in the world.

In the mansion on Cathedral Square
his patron tells the other kids to let him be,
in the solitude she calls *raptus*. She smiles
at his surly way of shouldering people off,
his fits of reverie, lost
in a re-tuning of the spheres.

I think of the flotation capsule, a time lapse
of dark water I paid good money to get shut into.
When the hatch came down
I heard nothing but my own heartbeat,
a ripple if I stirred
and rhythm patterns created by the mind.

This boy has no idea that before he's thirty
some inflamed wet muddle of labyrinth and cochlea,
thin as a cicada wing, will clog his ears

with a whistling buzz, then glue them into silence.
That he'll not hear music, except in the inner sanctum
neural pathways are preparing in his brain.

He knows he is different. He can do nothing about it
there is something inside
beyond the essential stirrings of the world.
Practising past midnight,
fingertips thickening, not noticing the cold,
what comes to him straight and true
as starlings flocking to a spill of corn

is how to dream new
when his fingers fly round a scale. He knows
what he can do is impossible for other people
but what's easy for them –
he spots it at flash moments, faced
with something he wants to say and doesn't know how –

is the gold caravanserai of the drawing-room.
Men in pigtails, women with high voices
speaking code he will never fathom.
It is all a dragon's lair.
Something he cannot understand
passes between one person and another.

The only thing he wants is to get his hands on the keys
and improvise
chord changes, clustering like the invisible core
of a galaxy whirling with planets.

Change key, swerve, change again,
make the piano sing to the heart of their nerves.

He holds
what he is given
forms of a chord progression
variation like a shining cloud.
He is sealed in himself, he is driven.
His hands are liquid. His hands are gold.

GROWING UP WITH BEETHOVEN

Sunday morning. My dad places crumbly sheets
of music on the stands. For the first time
we are meeting Beethoven. My eldest brother
with his cello, my sister on her violin –
she must be seven or eight – me on my viola.
But I'm mulish. I listen to Radio Luxembourg
under the bedclothes at night.
This music is inherited from Grandfather
who had to sign a document in the First World War
to say he wasn't German though he mainly was,
whose father was a concert pianist, taught
by a pupil, a follower, of Beethoven.
When I go to stay, Grandfather makes me play the piano
blind, over velvet
laid on the keys to keep them white.

String Trio, G major, Opus 9.
First time I hear my viola's true clear voice,
more awkward for my stiff hand
than the free bird singing in my throat –
as if I were two beings, the soprano
soaring upward unafraid
and the shy voice of blending in –
but I can see Beethoven has given each of us
something different to say. Mischief and hope:
I like that. When we've stumbled through
our dad says this melody reminded Grandfather

of sunlight on green mountains. Today,
when I listen, I see my dad
ahead on a mountain slope, stopping to look at a map
or check out other mountains through his telescope.
Now so many people I love have died,
others lost in the wisps and fogs of Alzheimer's,
I'd like to hold on to that
    looking back
to us three struggling with the notes
and the other two listening, waiting their turn.
Here we are still, the five of us,
trying to get the counting right.

IN THE ORCHESTRA PIT

Who is waiting for us in the twilight?
I played viola in a student *Magic Flute*
and night after night
everyone laughed at the dragon I never saw.

Night after night from the orchestra pit
I heard the tenor crack the top note of his aria
as he swore to break the fetters
of an imprisoned girl. I liked to imagine Beethoven

as a young man playing this part
but night after night I missed
the battle of light and dark,
the dragon of despair

when all stars shudder and go out,
and our need for magical thinking –
how music takes you through water and fire,
restores you to love.

MEETING MOZART

Never mind a three-week winter journey to Vienna
on your own. You're sixteen, burning
to be taught by Mozart Mozart Mozart.
He looks like a fat little bird. Bug eyes, fidgety,
tapping his toes. When you play one of his sonatas
he's unimpressed. But something makes him say,

All right then, improvise. And at last he's caught.
*Watch out for this boy. He'll give the world
something to talk about.* But a message from Bonn
skewers you back. Your mother's ill.
Your dream of learning
from the one man you measure yourself against,
whose music drives your heart, is snatched away.

She waits till you return
to drown in the coughed-up dregs
of her own lungs. And for the one and only time
in what's going to be a life of illness
you get asthma. As if her breath,
the breath she cannot catch, has stolen yours.

YOU RESCUE YOUR FATHER
FROM JAIL

She passed away after much pain and suffering. Ah, who was happier
than I, when I could still utter the sweet name of mother and it was
heard?

Beethoven to Councillor von Schaden, Bonn, 15 July 1787

When your mother dies
it's the end of something in you too.

Your playing has to keep the family.
Your father shameless, sodden in the street.

You argue in police stations at midnight
to save him from disgrace.

You now have to protect
the man who savaged you.

THE MEMENTO

Beethoven was always in love, and usually much affected by the love he was in.

Dr Franz Wegeler, *Biographical Notes*

I like to think of him suddenly slowing down
on the orchestra's tour up the Rhine.
No lessons to give, no hustling. Three weeks under sail
against a current whirling north – to Paris
and the Elector's sister, held in house arrest.
The Terror has not begun. No one on board,
or in castles on the banks, could dream
their world might be undone. But his whole mind
is revolution. The wind of it, blowing in his face.
He's twenty, about to step into the fullness of his art.
Back home is loneliness and practice. Here
they all love him. Everyone's an actor or musician.
Laughter. Water-dazzle. Rose-fly sunsets
light as smoke. The actor-king of the voyage
appoints his court. Ludwig is scullion, has to clean
the kitchen, wash up after thirty people twice a day.

When I was twenty, on tour in France, in the viola
section of an orchestra, it was *Rhapsody in Blue*
then rustles in the dark beneath the stars. On tour
with a choir, at the Europa Cantat Festival, Namur,
we'd rehearse all day, sing the concert,
let our hair down after like a fall of butterflies.
There must have been romance. Say it was that singer

Magdalena. Let's put them in the palace grounds
after opera highlights for the nobles' dinner
in a long green avenue
slowly becoming dawn. On the boat,
as they drift back to Bonn, he kisses her again.
Later, in Vienna, he'll propose. She'll turn him down –

but for now the actor-king
presents him with a seal of pitch
for diligent fulfilment of his duties
attached to a faux certificate by thread
from the ship's rigging. He'll keep this all his life,
his only honour for anything not music.
Treasure from a golden voyage, long ago.

THE BOY ON DRAGON ROCK

Beethoven on the peak of the Drachenfels …

Gerhard von Breuning, *Memories of Beethoven*, note

Sunlight on the Rhine. Europe about to shatter.
I'm following his steps up a red-lit path
through autumn woods. He's one of the gods
and knows it. An arrow fletched with fire.
He's raging to be gone, staring at this river

muscling north to France, detonating
in revolution. I'm standing where he stood
under a ruined tower, watching the silver
artery of Europe gleam-curve east
and south towards the Danube.

He's grown up by this rip of water,
gagged on its ripeness, played in its mud,
clambered over roofs with his mother
to escape its flood. When he leaves
he'll never see it again except in dreams.

VIRTUOSO

My compositions are bringing in a good sum, it is scarcely possible for me to execute the orders. Only that jealous demon, my bad health, has thrown obstacles in my way.

Beethoven to Dr Franz Wegeler, 16 November 1801

CITY OF MUSIC

*Go careful in Vienna, Everyone ought to go careful in a city
like this.*

The Third Man (1949)

I recognise it and I don't.
We all bring our own baggage
to the city Beethoven raced back to,
tipping the coachman
for galloping through armies mustering for war.
City of cover-up, selfie-sticks and autumn light
that sparkles on the pavement. Through a café door
I hear *The Third Man*'s zither, conjuring
a Ferris wheel, an Iron Curtain coming down.
I lived here years ago, on a German course
that didn't take. When my dad visited
for a psychoanalytic conference
we met Anna Freud, looked into the face
of ancient myth. Now I'm back for Beethoven
I shut my eyes, blot out imperial façades, imagine
something lethal whiffing up between the cracks
of the city where psychoanalysis had to be born,
that twisted thread into the labyrinth, leading to
the violence at the core, inhuman at the heart
of the human. In a diner where they say
Beethoven once lived, we run into an office party.
What of the Minotaur, the rise of the far right?
You can't tell, says my friend. *In the 1960s
you'd have known. Today*

you can't make out who's fascist and who isn't.
I think of Beethoven, arriving on his own
with Europe on the brink. Battalions everywhere
between himself and home.

WHAT COULD GO WRONG?

Wig-maker. Silk stockings, 1 florin 40 kreutzers ... Chocolate and coffee for
Haiden and me.

Beethoven, Memorandum Book, December 1792 and October 1793

Pension Mozart. Outside my room,
a poster of Joseph Haydn – long face,
bleached wig, quill in his hand, a frill
of perfect lace. I imagine scruffy little Beethoven
coming for a lesson. They don't get on.
Haydn's nickname for him is Grand Mugul.
He won't write 'Haydn's pupil' on any title page.

He ditches the wig, has his hair cut short
and choppy like a Republican,
gets a name as a bewitching pianist,
the new bright star,
beats everyone in improvising contests.
People stare at his whirling fingers, tufts of hair.
He goes on tour – Leipzig Dresden Prague Berlin –

composes cello sonatas for the Prussian king,
returns with a gold snuff-box, writes a song
everyone wants to sing. He's flirting,
writing lines of Schiller
in girls' journals. He is a meteor,
glowing. What can possibly go wrong?

EARTHQUAKE

A temblor, a slow-slip earthquake,
an undetectable assault
on the ground beneath your feet.

You can't feel it. No one knows
a tectonic plate
is sliding miles below along a fault.

TO BE PLAYED WITH THE UTMOST DELICACY

*I have found out how to write quartets … But your Beethoven lives most
unhappily, in discord with nature and the Creator. The finest part of me, my
hearing, has greatly deteriorated.*

Beethoven to violinist Karl Amenda, 1 July 1801

My first quartet concert. I'm nervous as a foal.
I know nothing about Beethoven, have no idea
his first quartet is such a deal for him.

I don't know he's picturing the vault scene:
Romeo, when he finds Juliet dead.
Now I find

he wrote in his sketchbook, over the slow
movement, *He's getting near
the tomb. He kills himself. Last sighs.*

Four voices, each on their own wild ride.
A to-and-fro, an either-or, a yes-and-no.
A family conversation

like his father, brothers and himself
after his mother died. No one must know
his ears whistle, buzz, and sometimes block

all sound. Writing for four
has released him to the dark
mysteries of melancholy

as if sitting at the tavern, no one
knowing, has sparked
a slow-drip solitude

he will refuse, at first, to go down into
yearning for something more
than the alone he's made. Four

as a country dance. Funny, playful,
jaunty as a shot of vodka
savage as devil-jugglers in a cave.

Loneliness at the core
of *con brio*. Night vision
searching for a key, a theme, a door.

MOONLIGHT SONATA

We make the life we need.
The city's bells are muffled,
the sky is frozen copper.
You still can hear, sometimes.
Still win the improvising contests.

A sonata in C sharp minor,
quasi fantasia, like a blind girl
lit by moonlight she cannot see.
New melodies unfold from tiny seeds.
Euphoria, then *presto agitato,* manic rage.

The music of loss, of losing. Bass clef.
High treble only once
and in despair. Then the new
shocked calm of *Is it true.* Is this
what it sounds like, going deaf?

THE JEALOUS DEMON

My hearing has become weaker in the last three years – this infirmity was caused by
my bowels which, as you know, were already in a wretched state. I was often in
despair. The humming in my ears continues day and night …

Beethoven to Dr Franz Wegeler, 29 June 1801

Wondering about Beethoven's brain,
the improviser, the variations man,
I stare at diagrams of research
on rappers and jazz artists.

If you can't hear what you're doing
how do you make the darkness echo,
where does the newness go?
Doctors pour oil in his ears

bind poisonous bark around his arms
raise angry blisters to lance and drain
imaginary toxins. His shoulders
run with pus. He dreams

of galvanism and electric wire. He asks
for his grandfather's portrait
to be sent from Bonn.
May the dead protect him.

JULIE

My life is a little more pleasant, I'm out and about again, among people – you can hardly believe how desolate, how sad my life has been these last two years. This change was caused by a sweet enchanting girl who loves me and whom I love. After two years, I am again enjoying some moments of bliss. For the first time I feel that marriage could make me happy. Unfortunately she is not of my station – and – and now – I certainly could not marry now.

Beethoven to Dr Franz Wegeler, 16 November 1801

Like waking up with a diamond in your palm
and seeing the world through a veil of love.
He's thirty, she's his pupil. Eighteen. A countess.
Soft fingers brush his on the keys.

He is a midnight beekeeper gathering a swarm.
But always that splinter of ice in the heart
protecting the work, and the safety of not
being loved. Not now. Maybe some day.

HE TAKES ROOMS IN A COUNTRY VILLAGE TO REST HIS EARS

I came here with the hope of being cured.

Beethoven, *Heiligenstadt Testament*, 6 October 1802

The omens are good. A spa, a place of healing. May.
Blossom bright as paint. The sparkling Danube canal.
Vineyards in bud, blue needle of distant mountains,
a narrow lane, a low arch to a bakery, the croissant sign –
and that yeast smell
like the house where he grew up, beside the Rhine.
Carters untie his piano. A sweet-herb wind
slips by like life, shaking the grass.

This is enough. His rooms look over misty fields.
Bring on the water cure and healing baths.

That's how I imagine him arriving
as I get off the tram at the end of the line
in a sleepy suburb, browse my way
up Beethovengang
and follow his steps into the cobbled yard.
The past splits open. God invents curious
torture for his favourites. He's thirty-one.
Fate has swung a wrecking ball.

I'm walking into his place of zero sum
where he must cast himself as victim or as hero.

HUMAN FIRE

Music should strike fire in the heart of man.

Beethoven to Bettina von Arnim, 1812

You spend mornings composing, tossing away
old drafts in crumpled balls, then plunge
into veins of forest. The notebook
swings in your pocket. Inspiration springs
from shadow, thistle-chandeliers,
red nipples of wild haws. You are Prometheus
the benefactor, stealing flame
to give to humans. A Shiva ray
creating and destroying. You are defiance,
a golden razor, a regatta. Lucifer
falling and flickering
with the discipline of firebreak.
Melody and rhythm flow from the molten blue
of summer hills.
    But there's a coppery stain
on the rising moon. You know creation comes
with pain. The stolen gift draws punishment in its wake
and ends in the rock, the vulture and the chain.
You stride on through the woods. You believe
in freedom. Human fire, created out of clay.

TAKE THIS CUP FROM ME

We all need a place to store the darkness.
Sitting in the garden of this bakery-
turned-museum, his Gethsemane,
I gaze up at his window.
Soft serif trees in golden shadow

and a wall of words he copied out from Kant.
The starry heavens above, the moral law within.
I'm still reeling from the piano
with a megaphone on the lid
like a prompter's box, to amplify the sound,

a staff he held against a piano with his teeth
trying to hear through his cranial bone,
and headphones with buttons you can press
to monitor how much fainter he'd have heard
as the years went by. Plus the recipe for bread soup

he looked forward to on Thursdays, with ten eggs
he stirred in, throwing any that weren't fresh
at the housekeeper. These cock-eyed
domestic details, of a man who plunged
head-first into work whatever was on his mind

made it more precise again and again,
writing new parts for trombone from his bed
the very morning of performance,

flash me back to a man who carved wood and stone
and showed me how to live a creating life.

I was young. He was twenty years older.
I stayed with him for ten. After the first night
I went to my desk, wondering what happened.
He came round in the evening, said
what a beautiful day's work he'd done

because of me. I learned that creating comes
from need. Also surprise.
That you put yourself in the way of grace
and let the material lead. But there's also risk.
You must have chaos in you

to give birth to a dancing star.
He was the ring of fire I had to break out from.
I cleared the bedroom, slipped away.
But here I am in Beethoven's garden
still thinking about him today.

A FLUTE OF LILAC WOOD

For half an hour he could not hear anything at all and became extremely quiet and gloomy, though I repeatedly assured him that I did not hear anything any longer either (which was, however, not the case).

Ferdinand Ries, *Beethoven Remembered*

This summer drop from apple branches
could be from your heart, you've been here so long
and nothing's changed. You watch August sun
blunt points of pears, darken grapes to amethyst.
Pigeons bulge and fan on the roof in silence
as if you're seeing them through glass
then fly into evening mist. At night, the moon
blood-paints the sloping lane. Life against the odds.
Wistful faces of white stars. By day the hill glows green,
dapple-darkens in cloud-shadow, glows again.
Catspaws of wind on summer barley.

But leaves don't rustle, birds forget to sing.
Your friend hears a shepherd in the forest play
a flute of lilac wood. When he sees you can't hear
he pretends it's stopped, like an executioner
balancing the axe on a prisoner's neck
without breaking the skin.
You know he's lying. In your mind
you hear Papageno's pipes
before he tries to hang himself. Go closer.
Still no sound. Only the rushing stream –
or is this eardrum rubbish, a chaos in your brain?

UNTIL IT PLEASE THE FATES
TO BREAK THE THREAD

*O you men who think or say I am malevolent, stubborn or misanthropic, how
greatly you wrong me. You do not know the secret cause which makes me seem that
way. For six years I have been hopelessly afflicted, made worse by senseless
physicians, from year to year deceived with hopes of improvement. I must face this is
for ever. Doomed to loneliness, deficient in the one sense which should be more
perfect in me than anyone. I would have put an end. Only my art – impossible to
leave the world until I have composed all I feel called to make. So I endure,
wretched until it please the Fates to break the thread.*

Beethoven, *Heiligenstadt Testament*, 6 October 1802

Five full moons. Five waning moons.
Touches of chill in the autumn night.
Dying vine-leaves, purple
as the pulse vein in his wrist.
The woods yellow, then black and bare.
    The candle trembles in a draught,
shutters swing in silence
like the sea breathing through glass.
He cannot hear the driving rain.
But he's sketching a funeral march,
a symphony. *I have taken a new path.*

HERO

Real improvisation comes only when we are unconcerned with what we play, so – if we want to improvise in the best, truest manner in public – we should give ourselves over freely to what comes to mind.

Beethoven, *Sketchbook*, 1809

EROICA

All night I've been thinking of you careening down
to the underworld. Now, with the resilience of a dervish,
you rage back up from the depths and get a job
as composer in a theatre. The man you hoped to be
is disappearing into the horizon like a creature of sea-ice
but you are fire-dust, gold-flight
winching upwards into pure light, Napoleon
the liberator, conqueror of the Alps. Battles are being won
smashing windows all over the city
making old Vienna and the Hapsburg Empire
look like a study of life on the ocean floor
while you drive forward into a new-world dawn
thrilling with dissonance, calling up wild-steel angels
no one has met before, looking down
on volutes of the foyer as on a dying fire.
You are havoc on the brink, a jackhammer
shattering the night and soaring past world-sorrow.
Against everything that can happen
to you or anyone, you pitch experiment
and the next new key, ever more remote.

LETTERS TO JOSEPHINE

Dear, beloved, only J! A thousand voices whisper you alone are my beloved – I am
no longer – oh beloved J let us walk again on that path where we were often so
happy … Tomorrow I will see you, may heaven send an undisturbed hour when my
heart and soul meet yours.

Beethoven to Josephine Brunsvik, 1805

You are all the colours of his sky.
When your aristocratic mother
hustles you and your sisters up his stairs
and tells him to teach you all piano
he takes one look at your heart-of-anemone eyes
and promises himself no spark of desire
is going to bloom.

You are astonishingly beautiful

but that doesn't always make for happiness. At twenty
you marry a count your mother thinks is rich.
You have three children in three years. He dies –
and here's Beethoven at your door. You venerate
his music, but how can a countess live
with a commoner who is going deaf
and keeps an unemptied chamber pot under his desk?

I can hardly bear to read his letters to you

pouring out his heart, not knowing
that in two hundred years

everyone will be able to share this lightly, online.
He is tearing Napoleon's name
out of the title page of a symphony
because his hero, this man of the people,
has crowned himself Emperor,

he is writing *Fidelio*

and seeing it performed
to an audience of French soldiers
who have just captured a city
and who walk out of the theatre when they realise
his opera is not only the dream of a loving wife
rescuing her man
but the abuse of military power,

and all this time he is on fire for you.

This is when Napoleon first occupies Vienna
thousands of soldiers dead in the battle at Austerlitz,
mutilated veterans begging in the streets –
and brother Carl has to marry a pregnant girl.
Jealousy, disguised as moral outrage.
She will sully the name of Beethoven!
He writes the *Appassionata*, whose pain

may express his agony at going deaf

but you are in it too. He writes you a song –
'To Hope'. And a piano piece, his declaration of love.

Here's your – your – Andante,
says his smudgy writing
telling you how to play it. No one could wish
his delusion away, it is gold dust –
we might not have *Fidelio* without it –

but what was it like for you, Josephine,

reading this torrent? I walk past the green door
he passed through daily at Theater an der Wien,
and read the way you try to cool him. Words like *esteem* –
I recognise that moment when you have to say
Let's just be friends. But we have all been
on the receiving end, too. Your servant
will not let him in. He writes to you about his Mass in C –

suffering humanity, yearning for fatherly love,

something he never knew but can imagine
and when he's creating no one can hurt him,
not his father, not you. He doesn't say
he fell ill after, alone in his lodgings.
The wound of you will take time to heal.
He still dreams of knocking on your door
while you disappear from his biographies

like fog from a mirror.

You marry a no-good baron, have more children –
he takes them away. You have another child

with a maths teacher. By the end
you will have had, I make it, seven. Your mother
says these disasters are your fault. You battle
to get your children back, but die alone aged forty-two
the year Beethoven writes his last piano sonata

which some people hear as your requiem.

You are lost in the milky blues of history.
So many men loved you, condemned you, wrote
books supporting or opposing your claim –
though you didn't claim –
to be Beethoven's Immortal Beloved.
Your life was a song to hope
and the dark crystal of desire.

What can we say to a firefly lost in the fire?

THE SHADOW BEHIND THE DOOR

Ramparts of Vienna. An airy view
Beethoven loved. The rooms
where he wrote the 'Archduke' Trio
and re-wrote *Fidelio*.

Nothing gave him such trouble.
I once asked a professional
singer what it was like
singing the First Act quartet on stage.

She said, *The earth moves if you get it right.*

On display, a showcase all to itself,
the canister that held his salt and pepper
rescued at an auction of his things.
Separate lids, delicately hinged

for each gilded compartment, like tiny harpsichords
opening side by side. Amazing this survived.
He rarely picked up anything without dropping it.
Every domestic item knocked and broken.

In shadow behind the door, a sign
says this museum was set up

in 1941.
Newspapers complained –

Jews, living in the house of Beethoven! –

and the family living here
was sent to Theresienstadt,
then Auschwitz.
I think of fallen stones, a Jewish cemetery

in forest overgrown by fern,
and the story of a cantor's son I heard
in Sejny, Poland. Twelve. Fastest runner
in the school. When the Nazis came

his father said *Run,* he ran the stretch
marked out on sports day, from
the synagogue steps to the forest edge.
The only one in town who got away.

This sign behind the door is Europe too.
We are all Vienna, the beautiful
city you cannot trust.
We know it now, know it again,

creatures of division, evil and good
blown off course by a bitter wind
and lost in a haunted wood.
We are the dark. Rift in the lute,

fault in the bone, the light
of enlightenment driven away
by monsters at the heart
and fallen feathers in the dirt like warnings.

But earth still moves if you get it right.

WINE OF THE HEART

When I was small I was sometimes allowed
to stay up when my father played quartets.
He gave his friends a glass of sherry first.

I remember him wiping little glasses,
opening music stands, opening the door
to the Iraqi violinist he played with before we were born

who was weak now, had to prop his elbow
to hold a violin. My dad put cushions under his arm,
offered a little wine. He couldn't drink, he said.

Wine of the heart, he said, gazing up with his dark
burnt eyes. The names of where these players came from,
Ljubljana Hungary Germany Iraq,

were as much a part of the grown-up world
as the peppermints my father kept
in the glove pocket of our first car,

a fawn Ford Popular, to help him give up cigarettes.
I learned that music comes from everywhere.
That it takes strength to hold a violin,

that music crosses languages
and is mysteriously connected
to what we feel

and never say, because my father worked
in hospitals of the mind
and was often away.

I remember sitting on the floor
watching his face as he played his cello.
I learned that music is love,

an echolocation
which falters or explores
across a cave of unknown distances

most safely entered by music
and summed up in the black and white photo
of my dad with his sister, brothers, parents

sitting by their music stands. Granny
with her viola, which I inherited,
Grandfather with his violin. My dad is eight

pointing to the music with his bow
and a white bust of Beethoven
glowers on a pedestal above.

I picture my dad's quartet at work
on Razumovsky Number 1.
He has the opening tune. I know he's anxious

to play it well. Maybe I'm still
anxious for him, even now after he's died,
as I stand in the evening light of old Vienna

looking up at the room where Beethoven tried
to knock a hole through the wall
and make a new window, so he could see the hills.

STAINED MANUSCRIPT

Prince! What you are, you are by circumstance and birth. What I am, I am through myself. There have been and will be thousands of princes. There is only one Beethoven.

Beethoven, note to Prince Lichnowsky, 1806

A daylight moon, watermarked with grey dapple.
I stare at the façade of the White Chateau, Silesia.
The castle of Hradec nad Moravicí
where Beethoven will shatter a long relationship
with the prince who was like a father to him.
Tall trees above a river. Berries ripen in the wilderness.
Indoors, gilt ceilings glitter. Privilege! He hates all that.
His opera has failed, he's lost his love,
he's furious with his brother, jealous of his brother's little son,
and deafer, always deafer. He will not play at dinner
for the enemy. I see him lift a chair
to strike his host, stamp away in a thunderstorm
through black salt of an October night
down this same gravel drive.
This is where it happened – eight miles
in shaking forest, lamé lightning, lashing rain.
He catches fever, shivers till the morning coach.
His bag, his manuscripts, are soaked.
Sometimes, in catastrophe, you have to slam the door
and save what you've made as best you can.
He shows his friends the music: waterstains
like scars on a country terrorised by war.

ON CUSHIONING YOUR EARS
IN A BOMBARDMENT

Sun rises on a frightened city. Shadows gather
on high horizons. Those who can, leave.
The rest stay: night watchmen, sausage sellers,
men who sell mousetraps, women who sell herbs,
bakers, washerwomen – and Beethoven,
up there in the line of fire. Napoleon
has rolled up at the gate at last.
Beyond the walls are twenty howitzers.

> *It was said that people milled around the streets*
> *swapping jokes to keep their spirits up, then went inside.*

Waving shadows. Kingfishers in speckled light.
I'm walking the Napoleon Trail
where his soldiers camped
on floodplain of the Danube.
Dogwood, willow, scattered gold. A path
between black poplars, an obelisk furred by lichen
on the site of his powder magazine,
where thousands of his men prepared the cannon.

As the light dies, Napoleon opens fire.
Beethoven hammers on his brother's door.
They take him to the cellar,
give him cushions to press over his ears.
There they stay, all night
and all next day. Brother Carl,
his wife Johanna and the baby,
two and a half. The little boy.

THERESE

*Since I cannot see her today, remember me to her and all of them – I feel so happy
with them, as though they might heal the wounds inflicted on me by wicked people.
Thank you, kind G, for having taken me there. Farewell, love me, your Beethoven.*

Beethoven to Baron Gleichenstein, 1810

I feel I'm seeing her in a rear-view mirror.
I know what it's like to persuade yourself into love.
He's desperate: in the silks of her father's drawing-room,
a man of forty picturing his life turned round

by a beautiful rich girl of eighteen. He asks friends
to lend a looking-glass for the afternoon, send
his birth certificate from Bonn, buy him neckties
and fancy linen, which some top tailor can fashion into shirts.
He's walking on air, picks out a piano for her,
gives her a copy of Goethe, writes her a tender bagatelle.

Friends worry he's heading for a fall.
The evening he plans to propose – so sure he's not alone,
she feels it too – he's fumble-drunk. Incapable.
The family whisk her away to their country home.

LOOKING OUT OF A BACK WINDOW

Roar of Vienna traffic on the Ring. All day
I've been reprising last night's dream
of the sculptor I once lived with.

I dreamed he felt bereft. Said he stopped being an artist
when I left. I held him in my arms, his heart
like hammer taps, chipping me from my world into his.

I told him that I see, I shall always see,
with the eyes he gave, and that he hadn't stopped,
he wouldn't, ever. When I woke

I remembered he was buried yesterday.
I hear three downward notes, Beethoven's goodbye
to his patron leaving the city

and to his teacher, dead after the shelling.
I'm staring, as maybe Beethoven did too,
out of the back window

in the apartment where he wrote
Quartetto Serioso – lightning-struck,
angry, almost a joke

about confronting, about going on whatever.
Abrupt, experimental, as all of us are
in the end, as we face the end.

I look into the ravine of the inner court,
see the building's shadow on the opposite wall
and over my head a hawk in a sky of milk.

THE VULNERABILITY OF VIOLINS

Berlin. Winter, 1970. We're playing the *Pastoral
Symphony* and my bow skids across the strings
without a sound. I think I'm going mad. A luthier
in an old violin shop says the back is coming off,
sticks the viola together, tells me his father fixed
the violin Menuhin played
for his Berlin debut, 1929. I take my viola to Prague.
This is after the Soviet invasion: a second boy
has burned himself to death. I stay with a family,
the apartment could be bugged,
we speak the language of quartets,
Haydn Mozart Beethoven,
till they walk me round the city in the open.
Bridges, smoke, a river of fear –
                                    where today
it's *Beethoven Luxury Suites for a Romantic Getaway*
and an ad for *Prague Stag Parties*. A girl,
black-leather buttocks, handcuffed wrists.

I walk past iron gates to the famous alley
where three stone violins on a carved cartouche
join their necks in a drunken kiss, above a door
Beethoven walked through
aged twenty-five on a concert tour
with a violin that needed mending.
But I'm thinking of him later, forty-one,
in Prague for the last time.

1812. July. A beginning and an ending.
Napoleon marching to Moscow. Beethoven
checking in to Zum Schwarzen Ross,
'At the Black Steed', on the Graben. His last shot at love.

MEETING OF THE WATERS

While still in bed, thoughts thrust themselves toward you, my immortal beloved. I can only live wholly with you or not at all ... O continue to love me – never misjudge the most faithful heart of your beloved L.

Beethoven, Teplitz, 6–7 July 1812

It is unlike anything else. Wild swimming. The nub
of selves meeting, a conflux of two rivers,
black and gold. Nerve-ends, twisting together
underground. Each name touched and forgotten
in a time-really-can-stand-still
that shivers to the bone. Moralities dissolve
in each other's dark. The two of them
are a shaman's journey, a quest to the interior.
The kiss. A promise that may never be fulfilled
but is complete, each moment, in itself.

THE PENCIL

My angel, my all, my own self – only a few words today, and that with pencil (yours!) … Can our love persist otherwise than through sacrifice? Can you change the fact that you are not entirely mine, I not entirely yours?

Beethoven, Teplitz, 6–7 July 1812

She left it behind. It stayed
in the room, on the table
buried in the earth
of songs, manuscripts
unanswered mail
the hotel bill

his only piece of her
camouflaged

like a guilty secret
in the air of every day.
It travelled beside his heart
through the falling rain
and breakdown in the forest. It says
Never cease to love me. It says *Apart.*

FOREVER YOURS, FOREVER MINE, FOREVER US

*Never can another own my heart, never – never – O God why have to separate
oneself from what one loves – my life in Vienna is a miserable life – Your love makes
me at once the happiest and most unhappy. Only through quiet contemplation …
can we reach our goal to live together – be patient – love me … What longing with
tears for you – you – you my love – my all – farewell –*

Beethoven, Teplitz, 6–7 July 1812

Sometimes giving up what you love leads on
to everything you wanted in your life
but that doesn't mean it wasn't loss.

What remains is an echo, an afterglow
from a night with a woman he loves
maybe the only night he ever spent with anyone –

a letter from a man who broke down
on a midnight dash through a forest.
He was warned. He ignored the warning

he always does. A letter he maybe never sent
and nobody saw until he died
and it was found in a secret drawer.

A promise of eternal togetherness
a wishbone about to break
a letter of goodbye

from a man aching to be touched
walking away from what means most to him
except his art. Who wrote long after

to his publisher, *Farewell*
is said only from the heart
and when you're alone.

YOU MUST NOT BE
HUMAN

You must not be human, not for yourself, only for others. There can be no more happiness for you except within yourself, for your art.

Beethoven, *Diary*, 1812

We have arrested someone who will give us no peace. He keeps yelling that he is Beethoven but he's a ragamuffin. No hat, and an old coat.

Constable to police commissioner, Baden, 1821

PRAYER ON BURYING A FLAME

Winter evening. All Souls' Night
in St Ignatius Old Cathedral, Linz,
where he wrote his 'Equal' fanfares for the dead.

White walls, gold leaf, dark wood.
I'm thinking of him beneath these vaulted ceilings,
seeing these same fingerprints of light.

The town's façades – rose, turquoise, jade –
hair salons, pizza takeaways and little pharmacies
are all shut out. No one left except himself and God.

He's said goodbye to happiness. He's rushed down here
to stop this brother marrying. You can be the moon,
bright as you like, but still be jealous of the stars.

Alone in this fluent dark, I imagine four
gold voices, a family of trombones
sliding against each other

to purify souls in purgatory,
mark his funeral of love. Sorrow beyond despair,
calm as rays of sunlight in a wood.

This music will be played at his own funeral.
Shining instruments of the dead:
no more heroic fight

but resignation, sacred light. He's bereft,
heartbroken, aground,
pouring everything into pure carnelian of sound.

THREE DAYS

O God give me strength to conquer myself. Nothing at all must fetter me to life …
O terrible circumstances that do not suppress my feeling for domesticity but prevent
its realisation. O God, God, look down upon this unhappy B, do not let it go on
much longer in this way!

Beethoven, *Diary*, 1812 and 1813

We shouldn't be reading this. A self-help diary,
the voice of loneliness and struggle.
Nothing can stop him tipping into the abyss

afraid that everything he could create
will stay locked in for ever.
He doesn't know where to go or what to write.

He stays with a friend outside the city,
a paradise of elm and oak, cool mosses, sun,
and at night the blowing net of stars.

But he vanishes without a word.
They think he's left. Three days go by
and the music master tracks him down

to a corner of the grounds
huddling like a wolf crawled off to lick its wounds.
Trying, he explains, to starve himself to death.

GIRL ON A SOFA

Sensual gratification without a spiritual union is bestial, afterwards one has no trace of noble feeling but rather remorse.

Beethoven, *Diary*, 1816

Brothels? Probably. Everyone did.
His assistant once came for a lesson
and found him on the sofa with a woman.
He was backing out, but Beethoven
waved him to the piano –

Play something romantic! He played,
not looking at the sofa. *Something passionate.*
He played on, flowing the world to its end,
suspended cadence, slow trill, *presto* –
till the girl departed.

The master had no idea who she was.

She knocked on the door, asking to see him.
He said it happened often. He was prudish
but enquired about a book on syphilis
and had a running joke with a friend
about *storming the fortress*.

INDIA DREAMS

You are even more alone. Ear trumpets
don't help but you pretend they do.
Glass filled with the moon's dry wine,
your shadow soft on the ceiling,
a moment when every silence in the world
conspires with every other

you write out notes of the Indian scale, read Hindu
mystics and *Shakuntala*, copy advice
given to a faithful wife, searching for
a husband cursed to forget her, on how to endure.
    On your journey through this earth
    your path will be now high, now low.
    The traces of your feet will be uneven.
    Virtue will drive you on.
Giving up on Eros and his blindness
you cleave to Brahma, the one bright eye,
a single coin of light opening in the dark
of pagodas you picture on mountain peaks, in India.

What we forget makes us who we are.
Most of our life vanishes in the swirls
of the brain's mysterious mirror
but you can't stop looking back. At scarlet pearls
strewn through the desert, footprints of blood,
your journey away from love.

TO THE DISTANT BELOVED

… a woman he would have considered union with the greatest happiness of his life.
It was not to be. He said he could not get it out of his mind … The new song, 'An
die ferne Geliebte', drew tears from my eyes. This can only have been written from
the heart!

Fanny Giannattasio del Rio, schoolmaster's daughter, *Diary*, 1816

Now she is far enough away
your heart can say what it wants.
Just as the winding stream
   meltwater starless rivers
carried on flowing all winter
under whistling silks of snow
when everything was a frozen dream

though when random flurries stirred
you could imagine soft little paw-prints
a feather imping the surface
   white on white
through processions of black trees

… but the ice is relaxing now,
plates of it jostle near the banks
riding the flow
of water dark and alive –

and now she is far enough away
your heart can break through, say

what it wants. The world is fluid
not fixed. It is as if she has died

carried on flowing all winter

and you can turn her into harmony
no matter if this is the flood
of remembered love
or the fire of making new.

THE BATTLE FOR KARL

The effort to save my dear nephew from his depraved mother was a heavy strain …
The Queen of the Night must not be allowed to see him.

Beethoven to Countess Erdödy, May 1816, and to Giannattasio del Rio,

schoolmaster, July 1816

You're not working. You're a mountain king
waylaid in your own black corridors.
You've quarrelled with old friends
horrified by your going to law
to tear your little nephew from his mother,
make him yours. This is a family romance
gone terribly wrong. You spend hours
writing to the court, to say
she is Queen of the Night, the mistress of pretence.
You are freezing over, going up in smoke, lost
in a labyrinth of fantasy
while a child waits backstage
for rescue. You are his true father. Your task
is to raise him to manhood. He shall be blest.

FIRST ENTRY
IN A CONVERSATION BOOK

This doesn't follow, that I should eat sausages the way you do.

Karl, *Conversation Book*, 27 February 1818

I love that the very first entry, Karl,
in the *Conversation Book* begun by your deaf uncle,
is you standing up for yourself. For a single man
who counts exactly sixty coffee beans, no more
no less, who has never lived with anyone without violent rows
and stormings out, it must be a shock
to see you say you won't eat sausage his way.

There is more of his own father in him than he'd like.
You are his sweet boy,
a poisonous ungrateful scamp.
He adores you, hates you, shakes you,
pushes you over so your little hernia pops out.
But you, at least, will come out the other side, go on
to have a wife and children, although you too

will die of cirrhosis of the liver, which suggests
an alcoholic vein runs into you from your great-grandmother.
But maybe what will turn you to drink will be trying to forget
what happened to you as a child. How you were torn
from your mother aged nine, the minute your father died,
locked up in boarding school while lawyers argued,
forced to give evidence against them both.

He is learning that wanting something does not make it real,
that nothing in this world is more difficult than everyday love
and that confusing real with ideal never goes unpunished.
He is standing on a hill of evil counsel. But keep on, boy,
this is going to end in devastation but somehow,
through all this muddle, something close to divine
revelation through music will be given to the world.

IN THE LYDIAN MODE

Holy song of thanksgiving of a convalescent to the Deity, in the Lydian mode.
Beethoven, over third movement of String Quartet, Opus 132, 1825

Cloud iridescence. Song like a book on optics
smuggled out of prison. The Milky Way
beyond a thatch of flame. Raw edges of a wound
coming together. God will find the pattern if you don't.

Self-portrait in chorale. Intimacy smouldering to blaze.
Wave-shadow like mourning ribbon,
honeycombs spilling honey, antiparticles
in outer space. Five wild points of light

unstable as the men outside the window
dismantling scaffolding
they've spent their lives depending on.
Panther eyes in undergrowth. Ultraviolet ash,

melody like flying jewels. Lightning
connecting earth and sky. The hope of figuring
what to hope for and to live inside that hope.
A place to lay the feathers and dust of yesterday.

Memories of your earliest wish: a world
where every soul will have fair turns.
A hermitage, a ghost of sunrise
where the sky brushes a sea aglow with grace,

and calm as the mist above it, wakening
the newborn blue of heaven. Quiet as a wreath of sleep
for anyone in sorrow. The slow unfold at last
of a promise that everything will be laid to rest,

every falling cadence in its place. A holy city,
a halo of gold leaf, saying tomorrow
is a mystery, today is a gift from God.
Without the dark we'd never see the stars.

ON OPENING THE MANUSCRIPT OF OPUS 131 IN THE MUSIC ARCHIVE, KRAKÓW

*While composing the three quartets such a wealth of new ideas flowed from his
imagination that he had to write the Quartets in C sharp minor and F major too.
'My dear fellow, I've just had another idea,' he would say jocularly with glistening
eyes, out walking, and write a few notes in his sketchbook.*

Karl Holz, violinist

(I)

Blue placard in a leafy street. The ordinary trance
of morning light on flickering poplars, windblown jade.
Bentwood chairs with metal legs. Pine desks.
Bound manuscripts with marbled covers.
I never believed I'd meet him here. Still less
that my fingers could touch his touch on the page.

(II)

Another chance to be new again.
Does being deaf break the chains?
Could he have written this otherwise?
Fugue and variation lead

to rebirth, regeneration,
the initial theme transformed
into a thousand petioles and branches
all carrying the DNA of the first seed.

(III)

Black cobweb crossings out. Five sharps
like wriggling insects. I can't imagine
how any player could read this
but I recognise the voices. First solo,
then together. Now angry and loud,
now gentle. I remember my father
saying you could tell from this
everything of the human.
Yearning, loving, in despair – then calm.
Amused and jokey, *sotto voce*, beyond loss.
Three bars slashed out. The way he wrote
espressivo. Here, over pale lines of the stave,
the famous tortured entries one by one.
When the librarian isn't looking
I kiss the corner of the page.

THE RAUHENSTEIN RUINS

I did it because my uncle harassed me.

Karl, report to police, Vienna hospital, July 1826

He's never climbed these battlements alone.
Only with his uncle, whom he refuses to call Father
but who insists on calling him his son, and sets a crazy pace
up these broken steps as if he owns the place.

In autumn these trees cascade like blood
from pinnacles of rock. He's never been here
in winter. He'd love to see the damn thing
smothered in snow. Sometimes they've come in spring

when the fortress ring is spotted with green buds,
but mostly in summer, like today
when the ruined windows stare unbroken blue.
He used to think if he did what Uncle said

he would be safe. But nothing's safe
around his uncle. Everything's a fight.
Uncle shouts for hours saying what he's done wrong.
He shouts back the suspicions are not true.

The letters that come after, saying *my sweet boy*,
don't make any difference. Just the same next time.
He's a prisoner in Uncle's dungeon, a broken
castle in himself. Blood of the sun,

blood of the moon. He'll never get away
except like this. When Uncle finds,
as he soon will, how a father damages a son, he'll cry.
He'll be sorry the rest of his life, and serve him right.

BREAKING AXLE

Why are you making such a scene today? Will you not let me go a little now? I only want to go to my room. You must realise other people are human too.

Karl to Beethoven, Gneixendorf, *Conversation Book*, October 1826

On my screen is the château
where Beethoven is finishing his last quartet
staying with his brother
and the sister-in-law he hates
near a village whose name,
he says, sounds like a breaking axle.

Here he is, dropsical, all diarrhoea
and swollen feet, holding in his gut
with a truss, at his desk
above the garden
looking down on a sundial
inscribed *Memento Mori*

and I'm there with him, plummeting into the past
to find some blessing in it. When he plays duets
with his nephew, I make sure
he enjoys it. I want him to glide
through his only close relationships
like a falling star

and not accuse Karl of sex with his sister-in-law
just because the boy plays duets with her too.

I am trying to cancel
the mathematics of strain,
and give his brother enough money to pay the mortgage
so he does not press Beethoven for rent.

If Beethoven looks like flying into a temper,
ordering a servant to drag out
an open milk-wagon
and take him and Karl back to Vienna –
a two-day December journey
staying the night in an unheated inn

falling so ill he'll have to be lifted on the cart next day –
I shall make this not happen. And if it does
I'll call out in the forest
from dark lanes dusted with snow
for them to keep each other warm, he and Karl,
heads on each other's shoulders,

two hearts tilting into each other
like drips of light in a breaking rainbow
for there is love here, this is the last time
they will be alone, Karl is the one
person he has tried to live with and love long term
and I don't want him to have screwed it up completely.

I will take a shot of him not screwing it up
on my phone. And before they leave
in a midnight blur of recriminations
here is a shot of him in that house

in his last months of active life,
the ghosts of grief

in caverns of his psyche
letting him down lightly. But no,
I see him drinking even more heavily
and nagging – he will not let his nephew be,
even for a second – so I call his name.
Ludwig! Herr Beethoven! *Bitte!*

He turns, he smiles. He says, Ruth,
will you take the parts I have just copied out
of my new quartet, with a joke in them
about accepting mortality, to my publisher in Vienna?
He hands them over. I think I probably bow
and I say, It will be an honour.

MUSICA HUMANA

*I still hope to create a few great works and then, like an old child, finish my earthly
course somewhere among kind people.*

Beethoven to Dr Franz Wegeler, December 1825

The auditory canal
covered in glutinous scales
shining throughout the autopsy

the auditory arteries
thick and cartilaginous
as if stretched over a raven's quill

and the auditory nerve
withered
to a pure white strand.

But reading the last page
in the book of his life on earth
how he joked

to the doctor who lanced his belly,
gallons of fluid gushing across the floor,
You remind me of Moses striking the rock with his staff

how he laughed, when he could, how he read
and re-read – with great joy, he said – a final gift,
a forty-volume set of all the works of Handel

and how he died
lifting his fist
as if it held a bird he would release into the storm

pelting Vienna with snow
like the reckless feathers driving all our lives
to seek the fullest experience of the air,

    I listen to Cello Sonata Opus 69
    and hear the unquenchable spirit
    that powers every note he writes

and lives on
dancing, dancing
in you, me, everyone.

LIFE-NOTES

A CODA

Music in the Dark of the Mind

Beethoven was born in 1770 on 16 or 17 December. In Bonn, in an attic on Bonngasse, a street of tradespeople – which meant musicians, too. The landlord was a lace-maker who lived on the lower floors. The house is now the Beethoven-Haus, a study centre and museum. His mother Maria had two more boys, Beethoven's brothers Caspar Carl and Nikolaus Johann. Of her seven children, these three were the only ones to survive.

As a toddler, the person Beethoven adored was the Flemish grandfather he was named after. Louis or Ludwig van Beethoven was Music Director at the Bonn Elector's palace, a singer who traded wine on the side. When his wife became alcoholic, he placed her in an asylum. He was critical of his son, Johann, but proud of his little grandson, and died when Beethoven was three.

Johann, a court singer like his father, though not as talented, became alcoholic like his mother. He pawned his father's court portrait; Beethoven later rescued it and put it on the wall everywhere he lived.

When Beethoven's grandfather died, the family moved into his apartment in a house belonging to a baker's family, the Fischers. The boys played with the Fischer children. The house has gone, but the Rhine is still at the bottom of the street. One year it flooded; Maria led the children to safety over the roofs. One Fischer child wrote a memoir remembering Beethoven laughing, getting up to mischief, looking through a telescope at the hills beyond the Rhine, especially the Drachenfels, which he later climbed (his love of country walks began early), and staring into space in a trance of concentration.

Johann recognised his son's gift, started him on violin, viola and keyboard at four, then hired better teachers. When Beethoven was around ten, Johann took him out of school and put him to work in the Elector's court orchestra playing viola, middle member of the violin family. In the Beethoven-Haus, you can see the viola he played. Many composers have played the viola. It does not have the brilliance of the violin or power of the cello, but when playing it you hear everything going on around you, all the relationships and harmonies, from inside. It is a writer's instrument, inward and between.

But Beethoven's great instrument was the keyboard. (Not quite a 'piano' yet: keyboards were changing and he himself later contributed to the evolution of the fortepiano.) His teacher was Christian Gottlob Neefe, court organist, head of the Bonn lodge of Illuminati, a Mason-like society whose humanist ideals fired Beethoven all his life. Schiller's 'Ode to Joy' was often set to music at their meetings.

By twelve, Beethoven was a keyboard virtuoso, renowned for doing exactly what his father reputedly punished him for, early on: improvising. Close to his improvising genius lay his insight into variation. One form of variation, constant development of a theme, would become a central feature of all his work.

His life changed at thirteen when Franz Wegeler, a medical student friend, introduced him to the von Breunings, a rich and cultured family. He taught piano to several of the children, became a favourite there, and sometimes stayed the night. He later called the whole family 'guardian angels of my youth'. One son, Stephan, became a lifelong friend. The widowed mother, Helene von Breuning, tried to teach Beethoven good manners and labelled his intermittent trance of concentration his 'raptus'. She introduced him to poetry, to other houses where he could earn money by teaching piano, and to people who helped his career, above all a well-connected young aristocrat, Count von Waldstein.

When Beethoven was fourteen, the Bonn Elector died. The Elector usually belonged to the Austrian Emperor's family and the new one was a friend of Waldstein's: in 1787 he gave permission for Beethoven to go to Vienna, to study with Mozart. But within a few weeks Beethoven had to return to his dying mother. Johann went to pieces when Maria died and Beethoven, now aged sixteen, had to keep the family by his playing and teaching.

In 1789, the French Revolution began. Like other enlighten- ment idealists, eighteen-year-old Beethoven supported it. Though he grew up wearing the court orchestra's uniform and later depended on moneyed patrons, he was always fiercely against inherited privilege. In February 1790, the Emperor died. Beethoven was commissioned to write two cantatas: a funeral cantata for the old Emperor, a coron- ation cantata for the new one.

The following year, the Elector ferried his orchestra and actors up the Rhine for a month of concerts. A soprano on that tour (who met Beethoven a few years later in Vienna) told her niece he proposed to her but was 'half-crazy and too ugly'. Beethoven, however, remembered the trip as a 'source of loveliest visions' and the 'seal' he was given then, in fun, was found among his things when he died.

In December 1791, in Vienna, Mozart died. Beethoven had lost his chance of studying with the composer he most revered, but Haydn travelled through Bonn in July and Beethoven showed him his cantatas. Haydn was impressed: Waldstein encouraged the Elector to let Beethoven go to Vienna again, this time to study with Haydn. At twenty-one, on All Souls' Day, 2 November 1792, with a French army heading towards Bonn, Beethoven left town and never returned.

Virtuoso

In Vienna, Beethoven began studying with Haydn, though he took lessons from other composers too. The day after his twenty-second birthday, his father died in Bonn. Busy making his name as a pianist, he stayed where he was and left his brothers to clear up after his father's death.

He was invited to move into the mansion of a great music patron, Prince Lichnowsky. After a few years he found living there oppressive and moved out, but carried on playing at Lichnowsky's private salons, and in those of another rich patron, Prince Lobkowitz.

In January 1794, Haydn left for London. Like fizz released from a bottle, Beethoven wrote three piano trios, his first numbered publication, as well as two piano concertos and three sonatas. He also started his First Symphony.

In March 1795, Lichnowsky arranged for Beethoven to hold his first public concert in Vienna's Burgtheater. Beethoven was twenty-four. His stomach hurt, a problem that would always plague him before concerts. Two days before, he was still writing the concerto he intended to play; copyists finished orchestral parts the morning of the concert. All his life he would write up to the wire. But the concert was a success, and Mozart's widow asked him to play a Mozart concerto in public. He had arrived.

Haydn returned in August and criticised the third, the most original, of the new piano trios. Beethoven stopped lessons with Haydn but dedicated to him his Piano Sonatas Opus 2, and on his deathbed was delighted to be gifted a picture of the house where Haydn was born. 'Such a little place,' he said, 'for such a great man.'

Napoleon captured Bonn, and some of Beethoven's old friends migrated to Vienna. So did his brothers. They were now using their middle names. Caspar, a mediocre musician, was now Carl. Nikolaus, a pharmacist, was now Johann, their father's name. Carl got a clerk's job in a government Finance Department but for some years worked also as Beethoven's agent. Publishers disliked him. When Carl sold to one publisher a piece Beethoven had promised to another, the brothers came to blows. Beethoven idealised the bonds of family, but his relations with his brothers were always fraught.

Beethoven wrote a popular song, 'Adelaide', and went on a European concert tour. Somewhere around 1796, the story goes, he stripped off after a long walk and stood sweating in a draught, which set off a bout of illness, possibly 'typhus'. This began, unperceived at first, to affect his ears.

He kept playing quartets, the form which Haydn invented and Mozart made more dramatic. He often played with a myopic cellist, Baron Zmeskall, who worked in the Hungarian Chancellery and smuggled him quills to write with from the office. When Beethoven too had to wear glasses to read music, he wrote for Zmeskall *Duet for Viola and Cello with Two Obbligato Eyeglasses*, a playful piece that shows him thinking hard about string chamber music: the two voices are equal. In 1798, he wrote the Opus 9 String Trios my father introduced us to as children; and then Prince Lobkowitz commissioned him to write six quartets. Beethoven soon finished the first, Opus 18, No. 1, and gave a copy to his violinist friend Karl Amenda.

But he took his time with these quartets. He studied those of Mozart. He had grown up playing viola, but his virtuoso instrument was the piano. Three years later he asked Amenda not to lend out the draft he had given him, as he had re-done it. Amenda said the sorrowful Adagio reminded him of lovers saying goodbye. Beethoven was pleased: he said he'd been thinking of the tomb scene in *Romeo and Juliet*. But that scene is hardly lovers saying goodbye: Juliet is dead and only Romeo's feelings matter. The pain is that of a young man alone and bereft in the dark – as Beethoven, through the three years he worked on these quartets, was alone with the dark secret of his deafness.

But he did go to doctors. In November 1801, he wrote to Wegeler of 'blistering plasters' placed on both arms. They were meant to draw out 'toxins' that blocked his ear ducts. 'A most unpleasant cure. I am deprived of the free use of my arms, to say nothing of the pain. I cannot deny that the humming with which my deafness began has become somewhat weaker, especially in the left ear. My hearing, however, has not in the least improved.'

Often, now, he couldn't hear musical notes, or what people said. Brain research on jazz musicians shows that while improvising they shut down their frontal lobe, the censor which inhibits expression, and switch on the medial prefrontal cortex, which releases imagination. Beethoven, the great improviser, must have done that too, but now he could not always hear the sounds he produced. How would that affect things? All six Opus 18 quartets express vivid emotions – joy, sadness, fear, playfulness – but the last is on a new, more tragic plane. He named its final movement 'La Malinconia', and marked it, 'To be played with the utmost delicacy.' Its anguish, quick changes of mood and unstable harmonies foreshadow the late quartets and must reflect his terror at what was happening.

But he was also discovering that writing for four voices in the same tonal family, a structure strong enough to contain instability, disagreement, ricochets of feeling, all the stuff that goes on in a family, was the perfect form to express internal conflict and resolution – all the stuff that goes on in a psyche.

While he was writing the quartets, Lichnowsky started paying him an annual allowance and gave him four valuable seventeenth-century instruments: two violins, a viola and cello. In April 1800, Beethoven put on his first 'benefit' concert, fundraising for himself: a public concert showcasing the First Symphony and instantly popular Septet. In the audience was his future patron, the Emperor's youngest brother Archduke Rudolph, a keen boy of twelve.

His professional life was flourishing. He was commissioned to write the music for a successful ballet, *The Creatures of Prometheus*. But in the summer of 1801 he wrote a piano sonata he called *Sonata quasi una fantasia* (later known as the 'Moonlight' Sonata because it reminded a German poet of moonlight on Lake Lucerne), whose turmoil may express his despair at going deaf. Then he fell in love with an eighteen-year-old countess, Julie Guicciardi, whom he met through her cousins, his pupils Therese and Josephine Brunsvik. He taught Julie piano, dedicated the 'Moonlight' Sonata to her and possibly proposed. But she preferred a count, whom she married the following year. She remembered Beethoven as 'noble and refined in feeling but very ugly'.

A young pianist, Ferdinand Ries, son of a violinist who helped the Beethoven family when their mother died, arrived in

Vienna from Bonn. He became Beethoven's devoted assistant, and later wrote remembrances of him. 'He was a thoroughly kind person at heart,' Ries said, 'but his temper and irritability got him into trouble.'

In May 1802, Beethoven despaired of doctors' attempts to cure his deafness. He followed the one sensible bit of medical advice he received, to 'rest his ears' outside Vienna, and rented rooms in a bakery in Heiligenstadt, a spa village an hour's wagon-drive out of town. This bakery is now a museum in a leafy suburb. It contains an old wooden bakery sign, the croissant, reflecting the story that Vienna's bakers saved the city in the Turkish siege and created a pastry memorialising the crescent on the Turkish flag. Perhaps the smell made Beethoven feel at home. His grandfather was a baker's son; the house where he grew up had been a bakery too.

This museum also displays, however, the desperate methods Beethoven used, as he grew deafer, to try to hear music. Placing a stick between your forehead and a piano, for instance, does work, a little: the cranial bone transmits soundwaves to the inner ear, hair cells on the cochlea convert them into electronic signals, and the auditory nerve is supposed to conduct these to the brain.

But we know from the record of Beethoven's autopsy that his auditory nerve was withering. He hadn't a chance, and Heiligenstadt was where he had to face it. He stayed six months, hoping his ears would recover. Eventually he had to accept that they would not.

Pieces he wrote there, like the 'Tempest' Sonata Opus 31, reflect his anguish, but also show a new style developing. His Fifteen Variations and Fugue in E flat are known as the 'Eroica' Variations because he used their theme later in the *Eroica Symphony*, which announced his new 'heroic' style. But he created that theme for his Prometheus ballet music and they could just as well be called the 'Prometheus' Variations.

Prometheus was a Romantic symbol of creativity through revolution. Fire, which he stole from the gods, was also creativity itself – a divine prerogative. His revolution was to give it to human beings and suffer for it. Contemporary painters portrayed his punishment in vivid detail: chained to a rock with an eagle eating his liver.

The 'Eroica' Variations were revolutionary too. When writing a 'theme and variations', the convention was to state the theme first, but Beethoven *began* with variations. Even more unusual, variations in the bass. He was working from the ground up, as Prometheus created human beings from clay, as small flames flicker into fire. He wrote to the publishers Breitkopf & Härtel, 'I have written variation works in a truly new manner. Usually I only hear others mention when I have new ideas, since I never know it myself, but this time I have to reassure you that the manner is entirely new.'

These pieces suggest his heroic style evolved partly out of his genius for variation. And also that behind the *Eroica Symphony* stands not just Napoleon, but the ancient Greek hero of creativity, defiance and suffering. As if Prometheus lit the fuse for his blaze of creativity ahead. After returning to Vienna, Beethoven dramatised another lonely hero suffering on humanity's behalf. The late eighteenth century sometimes identified Prometheus with Christ, and Beethoven's Gethsemane oratorio, *Christ on the Mount of Olives,* premiered in April 1803.

But before he left Heiligenstadt, he wrote a document now called *The Heiligenstadt Testament.* It was discovered in his desk after he died, and begins, *For my brothers Carl and ... Beethoven,* as if he could not bear to write 'Johann', his father's name. It is partly a will, telling his brothers to be kind to each other, leaving them his precious string instruments, but reads like an open letter to all humanity, including us, his future listeners, the audience he knew he was writing for. It describes his agony at going deaf and says he thought of killing himself but has decided to live for his art.

This crisis of despair and decision collided with a chrysalis moment, a breaking of style. In his childhood he developed extraordinary resilience, and ways of protecting his music no matter what. What he had to protect and nurture now were the seeds of the *Eroica.* His first rush of creativity had been driven by tension between his classical roots and a restless search for new modes of expression. His style now changed dramatically. In a very short time, he was tackling new forms, and approaching old ones in new ways. Having rejected suicide, he embarked on the most creative period of his life.

Hero

In January 1803, he began living with his brother Carl at the Theater an der Wien, as resident composer. He was under contract to write an opera, but began with his revolutionary *Third Symphony*. At first he called this the *Bonaparte Symphony*, dedicating it to Napoleon who seemed to embody his democratic ideals. But in May 1804 Napoleon was crowned Emperor of France. Beethoven, furious and disillusioned, scratched out Napoleon's name. It is now known as the *Eroica*.

He also wrote his opera, *Fidelio*. Its imagery and themes – good and evil, light and dark, the rescue of a prisoner – reflect his love for Mozart's *Magic Flute*. *Fidelio* was to have a troubled history: first performed in 1805, revised but withdrawn in 1806 (Beethoven quarrelled with the theatre manager), not revised again until 1814. It opened in November 1805, just after Napoleon walked into Vienna unopposed. The Viennese stayed indoors; the audience was mostly French soldiers. Then, in December, Napoleon decimated the Austrian army at Austerlitz, dissolved the Holy Roman Empire, annexed parts of Austria, and turned German states like Bonn, formerly under Austrian rule, into the Confederation of the Rhine, governed by France.

In 1804, the husband of Countess Josephine Brunsvik, Beethoven's ex-pupil, died. Beethoven, a family friend, now fell in love with her. Her family worried: noblewomen who married commoners lost custody of their children. Beethoven's piano pieces *Andante Favori* and 'Appassionata'

Sonata throb with love for her, but drafts of her replies to his letters suggest she refused a physical relationship and when he dedicated the song 'To Hope' to her, she was angry that people saw the dedication: she wanted the relationship kept quiet.

Soon Josephine was not at home when he called. 'I went to your home twice – but could not have the happiness of seeing you,' he wrote. 'It hurts me – maybe your feelings changed – I no longer wish to be subjected to rejection by your servants – be frank – I deserve it – even if I suffer – is it true you do not want to see me any more?'

Josephine died in 1821, the year of his last piano sonata, Opus 111, in which some people hear 'her' theme from *Andante Favori*. Some scholars think she was the 'Immortal Beloved' addressed in his love letter of 1812. But in 1806, when he is thirty-five, what matters is that this is the fourth woman we know of, and probably the most important, to reject him.

In May 1806, brother Carl compounded Beethoven's heartbreak by marrying his own pregnant girlfriend, Johanna. Beethoven called Johanna immoral (she once accused a servant of stealing something she had stolen herself) and tried in vain to stop the wedding. Their son Karl was born in September.

The depth of feeling in what he was writing now must reflect many painful emotions: anguish over Josephine and his worsening deafness but also horror at the suffering he saw everywhere after Austerlitz. Yet these works are also full of confidence, excitement, ways of shifting sorrow into joy.

They include his second set of string quartets, Opus 59, commissioned by Vienna's Russian Ambassador, Count Razumovsky. Beethoven wrote them in six months; they seem to have strengthened his sense that the string quartet was a form in which he could express intense feeling with particular intimacy. 'I'm thinking of devoting myself entirely to this type of composition,' he told the publisher.

In late summer 1806, depressed by Josephine, *Fidelio*'s failure and Carl's marriage, he stayed with Lichnowsky in his Silesian castle. One night, Lichnowsky invited the leaders of the occupying French army to dine and ordered Beethoven to play for them. Beethoven refused. There was a very public row; Beethoven rushed back to Vienna with the manuscript of the 'Appassionata' Sonata and sketchbooks for the Opus 59 quartets, and smashed a bust of Lichnowsky which the prince had given him. He lost his allowance and relations with Lichnowsky never really recovered, though later the remorseful prince, almost bankrupted by the war, used to climb the four flights to Beethoven's rooms, sit outside and listen to him play. Beethoven never let him in.

In September 1807, Beethoven was commissioned by Haydn's old patron Prince Esterházy to write a mass. He said he felt trepidation, not a word he often used. He was entering his old teacher's territory: the mass would be performed at Eisenstadt, where Haydn had lived as court composer. Sketches show he studied Haydn's masses closely. He wrote a Mass in C, which the prince hated and privately called 'ridiculous, detestable'. He showed his dislike publicly, it was the worst humiliation of Beethoven's career and he left Esterházy at once.

But the response to this mass of the more discerning Viennese critic E. T. A. Hoffmann sums up exactly what Beethoven – post-Josephine, and increasingly deaf – must have felt while writing it; and also the way that though Beethoven the man often despaired, his music always turns sorrow into consolation, finding redemption in even the most tragic themes. The Agnus Dei, said Hoffmann, expresses 'An inner hurt which does not tear the heart but is good for it; and dissolves to unearthly delight, like sorrow from another world.'

Beethoven rented a flat in a building where his Bonn friend Stephan von Breuning, now a civil servant in Vienna, also lived. Their friendship went up and down. 'You wouldn't believe what terrible effects the decline of hearing has had on him,' Stephan wrote to Wegeler in 1804. 'Withdrawn, distrustful, often of his best friends, irresolute.' But Stephan, always loyal, suggested Beethoven move into his own flat to save money. Beethoven did, but failed to give notice to their landlord, who asked for his deposit back. The friends quarrelled and Beethoven moved out. They made it up, but Beethoven transferred his belongings to a fourth-floor apartment on the bastion, now another Beethoven Museum: the Pasqualatihaus, where he lived on and off for eight years.

This apartment had a view of the green belt round the city walls (dismantled in the mid-nineteenth century to make way for the Ringstrasse) but Beethoven wanted to see the

Vienna woods too and knocked a hole through the wall. His landlord, Baron Pasqualati, was furious and Beethoven had to leave. But he returned two years later, and this was where he lived longest; where he wrote, among other works, the Fifth and Seventh symphonies, 'Archduke' Trio, and the final version of *Fidelio*.

In 1808, he was offered a salary outside Vienna as Music Director at Kassel. In December, he held a benefit concert in the Theater an der Wien: the public premieres of the Fifth and Sixth (*Pastoral*) Symphonies, parts of the Mass in C, and himself playing his Fourth Piano Concerto. It lasted over four and a half hours, the hall was freezing cold, the audience tittered at the birdcalls in the *Pastoral*. This concert heralded the end of his performing career. He was too deaf to play. In January 1809, he accepted the Kassel offer.

Alarmed, his friends arranged a better deal with rich Viennese patrons. Beethoven would stay in Vienna composing whatever he liked, paid by an annuity from three noblemen: Prince Lobkowitz, Prince Kinsky and the twenty-one-year-old Archduke Rudolph, whom Beethoven was now teaching piano and composition.

So 1809 started well. Though too deaf to play his viola in tune, he wrote in a sketchbook, 'Quartets every week'. But in April, Austria declared war on France. Napoleon defeated an Austrian army, marched towards Vienna and established a base camp at Linz, where Beethoven's youngest brother Johann had an apothecary's shop. (Beethoven was now the only brother without property; Carl's wife had a house in Vienna.) Johann supplied the French army and its wounded soldiers with medicine. He became one of the richest men in Linz – and the most hated, for collaborating with the enemy.

Before Napoleon attacked, the Emperor's family left Vienna. Beethoven wrote a 'farewell' piano piece for Archduke Rudolph. He said it was the first movement of a sonata and he would write the rest when Rudolph returned. He often complained about the time he spent teaching Rudolph composition, but he valued Rudolph's musicianship (he asked him to play the piano in premieres of important pieces) and Rudolph's astonishing music library. He must have felt that of all his patrons, Rudolph best understood his work.

Over the first three downward notes of this piece, he wrote the word *Le-be-wohl*, 'Farewell'. He wrote an 'Absence' movement later, and a third, 'Return', when Rudolph came back. When the whole sonata was published, he scolded the publisher for titling it *Les Adieux* rather than *Lebewohl*.

During the siege, 10–13 May, a cannonball landed in Haydn's courtyard. The old man was unharmed but shocked. Beethoven, meanwhile, fled to his brother Carl's cellar. When Vienna surrendered, French troops entered and occupied the city. On 31 May, Haydn died.

Beethoven spent most of the occupation copying theory exercises for teaching Rudolph composition. Then he re-used his *Lebewohl* theme in a single string quartet, 'The Harp'. It sounds like a tribute to his old teacher, who invented the string quartet. You could hear its plucked strings as angels' harps, accompanying Haydn to heaven. It could be Beethoven's reflection on the classical tradition Haydn embodied. Or just a farewell, ending with a simple cadence.

After occupying Vienna, Napoleon finally defeated the Austrian army in a bloody battle on the other side of the Danube. In October, he signed a peace treaty and departed, leaving Beethoven, like everyone, much poorer. Food was pricier; the currency devalued fivefold.

In April 1810, Beethoven fell in love with Therese Malfatti, daughter of a rich merchant. He was introduced to her by an amateur cellist, Baron Gleichenstein, who helped him with practical affairs and was courting Therese's sister. Beethoven had dedicated Cello Sonata Opus 69 to Gleichenstein, to thank him for arranging his annuity. Now, excited by this double courtship, he tried to smarten up, was delighted when the Malfatti family dog followed him home, and wrote Therese a bagatelle.

He arrived one evening apparently planning to play this piece for her and propose. But, so the story goes, he drank too much to do either. When Therese died, the piece was found among her things. No one knows why Beethoven wrote *Für Elise* on it, rather than *Für Therese*. It became one of the most popular piano pieces anywhere: in the 1990s, its melody was the most downloaded ringtone in the world.

Gleichenstein was ordered to tell Beethoven he was not welcome at the Malfatti house. 'Your news,' wrote Beethoven, 'has plunged me from the heights of sublime ecstasy down into the depth. For you, poor B, no happiness can come from outside. You must create everything for yourself, in your own heart.' He wrote another stand-alone string quartet, *Quartetto Serioso*, Opus 95, full of anger, anguish, defiance and a kind of jokey despair. Like the 'Appassionata' Sonata and Florestan's dungeon aria, it is in the dark key of F minor. It was not a commission, he clearly had to write it, said it was never to be performed in public, and dedicated it to his chamber music friend Zmeskall. He also set three Goethe poems of tragic love.

Some of the desolation he was grappling with in 1811 comes over in a scribble in one of his sketchbooks: 'Cotton in my ears at the piano takes away the horrible ringing in my ears.' But professionally he was becoming a legend. Hoffmann hailed his Fifth Symphony as the beginning of Romantic music; he was commissioned to write music for Goethe's play *Egmont*, and met a friend of Goethe's, Bettine Brentano.

He also met Bettine's half-brother, Franz Brentano, and Franz's wife, Antonie. In autumn 1811, he began to visit Antonie regularly. The Brentanos normally lived in Frankfurt, but her father had died in Vienna and she was clearing his house. When she was ill, Beethoven comforted her by playing the piano. He wrote a song called 'For the Beloved', and gave her the score when she asked.

In June 1812, he wrote an Allegretto for Piano Trio for Antonie's ten-year-old daughter, dedicating it to 'My little friend Maximiliane Brentano, to encourage her in piano playing'.

In late June, he left Vienna to take the waters at the spa of Teplitz and stopped en route in Prague, to collect part of his annuity money.

He had been to Prague before, for concerts. In 1796, he had a violin repaired there. The sign of the luthier's craft, three violins for three generations of violin-makers, still marks the door he took it through. In 1798, he premiered his First Piano Concerto there. But this was a private visit. He arrived on 1 July, and two days later the Brentanos also turned up, bound for Karlsbad. That night, 3 July 1812, Beethoven failed to keep a business appointment. His apology note does not say why. Hotel registers, coach passenger lists and police records show he left Prague on 4 July and arrived next day in Teplitz.

From Teplitz, on Monday 6 July, he wrote a letter to a woman he called his immortal beloved. 'My journey was dreadful!' he wrote. 'They warned me not to travel by night and tried to frighten me but that only spurred me on – I was wrong! The coach broke down … Yet I felt the pleasure I always feel when I successfully overcome a difficulty.'

The letter is an emotional roller-coaster. At one moment, they have to live together; at the next, they have to part. But it does imply they spent at least part of a night together. It was found with the *Heiligenstadt Testament* when Beethoven died. He probably never sent it. For two centuries, scholars have tried to identify the woman. Many German-speaking scholars think she was Josephine Brunsvik. Most English-speaking scholars believe she was Antonie Brentano.

Antonie was definitely in Prague at the right time. But she was married, her husband was a friend of Beethoven's, and Beethoven was very high-minded. If Antonie was his immortal beloved, how did he square his morals with his love?

We shall never know, but this moment was his second supreme crisis. The difference between this and his crisis of facing deafness, ten years before, lies in his work. In 1802, the new form his creativity would take was already stirring. In 1812, he had reached the end of his 'heroic' style but did not see where to go next. It would be a long hard path.

You Must Not Be Human

He stayed on at Teplitz and started a diary. Loss and loneliness had to have a vent. He also did something he had longed to do: met Goethe. They talked for a week but it did not go smoothly. Beethoven disliked Goethe's deference to nobility; Goethe found Beethoven uncouth. 'An utterly untamed personality,' he wrote. 'I have never seen an artist more concentrated, energetic and intense. I can quite understand that his relationship to the world must be a strange one. He is not altogether in the wrong for finding the world detestable, but that does not make it more enjoyable for himself or others.'

Then Beethoven went to Karlsbad, staying in the same guest house as the Brentanos. We do not know what happened: they returned to Frankfurt but remained friends with him and in October Beethoven dashed off to Linz, to try to prevent another brother marrying. All his life, his family was entwined with his crises of loss. Each time he left Bonn for Vienna, he lost a parent. Each time he lost a woman he deeply loved, one of his brothers married a woman he was already sleeping with and Beethoven did all he could to stop him. Each time, he called the woman 'immoral'.

The woman concerned this time was Therese, Johann's house-keeper, who had an illegitimate daughter from a previous relationship. Beethoven stayed with them two months, tried to get rid of her, even made the Linz police order her to leave town. The brothers came to blows, Johann married Therese and later blamed Ludwig for his unhappy marriage.

While in Linz, Beethoven finished his Eighth Symphony. It is strangely light-hearted considering the turmoil he was in, though the manuscript is full of crossings out and scratchings that almost tear the paper.

He also made friends with Franz Glöggl, Music Director of Linz Cathedral. He asked to hear a Linz musical special-ity, played at funerals and on All Souls' Day: an *Equale*, in which instruments in the same family – trombones – played equally important parts. He then wrote Glöggl three new ones. 'Beethoven wrote me some mourning pieces for trombones. He wrote them in my room,' Glöggl wrote to Robert Schumann in 1838. A quartet for equal voices from the same family of instruments would have appealed to Beethoven's democratic instincts and his interest in quartets even in – perhaps especially in – the midst of a family row.

His *Equals for Four Trombones*, performed on 2 November, fore-shadow in miniature the sacred music he would go on to write, the *Missa Solemnis* and late quartets. They were played at his own funeral – and later, in England, at the funerals of Gladstone and Edward VII, where people praised their 'weird simplicity and exquisite pathos'. They were his first musical expression, perhaps, of his loss. Back in Vienna he wrote another: his last violin sonata, Opus 96. Then he entered the bleakest, most barren era of his life. Sustained, his diary sug-gests, by a sense of God experienced *von inner,* 'from within'.

Through most of his forties he was unhappy and isolated. Words like paranoid, alcoholic, depressed, psychotic, creep into biographies. He was a composer who was not really composing. In 1813 friends discovered him in Baden, 'So negligent of his person as to appear positively filthy, in a deplorable state. No decent coat or whole shirt.' At some point he tried to starve himself to death. Underneath, he was searching for another new path.

If he did visit brothels, it was probably during this period. The evidence is ambivalent but notes from him to Zmeskall, 1813–16, say things like, 'I am always ready for it, the time I prefer most of all is about half past three in the after-noon,' and 'Keep away from rotten fortresses [which seems to have been their code for prostitutes], an attack from them is deadly.'

1813 was also the beginning of Napoleon's downfall. The Eng-lish defeated French forces in Spain and an inventor per-suaded Beethoven to write music for a celebratory piece

involving an automatic playing-machine. He wrote the
'Battle' Symphony, a crudely populist parody of his heroic
style. It was his artistic nadir. He knew it. He told a critic,
'What I shit is better than anything you could think up.'

But in the same concert as the 'Battle' Symphony, the Seventh
Symphony was premiered and wildly applauded. The
Kärntnertortheater asked him to revive *Fidelio*. He revised
it again, it opened in May 1814, at last the success it ought
to have been, and was repeated the following year during
the Congress of Vienna. He had never been so fêted. Nor
so creatively at sea.

In 1815, brother Carl told Beethoven he was dying and had
nominated him joint guardian with his wife Johanna of his
nine-year-old son Karl. Beethoven demanded sole guard-
ianship and when Carl died was outraged to discover that
the will appointed Johanna the guardian, himself only
associate guardian.

'God permit my wife and brother to be harmonious for the
sake of my child's welfare,' Carl had written in his will, but
for the next five years Beethoven fought Johanna in the
courts for custody of her son. He wrote long letters to a
tribunal saying she was immoral; he nicknamed her Queen
of the Night, after the mother in *The Magic Flute*.

He knew he was being cruel. Old friends were shocked. He
told himself he was rescuing Karl. As, perhaps, he would
have liked to have been rescued from his own father. He
got sole custody in 1816, placed Karl in a boarding school
and visited at weekends. When Karl got low marks at

school, Beethoven punished him with coldness. Karl had a hernia operation: Beethoven did not attend. He made his pupil Carl Czerny teach Karl piano though Czerny said he had no talent. He swung between tortured tenderness ('my beloved Karl') and telling the schoolmaster to beat him if he did not work. Jealous that Karl went on loving his mother, he forbade Karl to see her; Karl disobeyed.

He was also still mourning his lost love. He copied into his diary advice about endurance through suffering, from the ancient Sanskrit drama *Shakuntala* (a German translation had just come out) in which a faithful wife loses the ring her husband gave her and wanders the world to find him – as Beethoven felt he was doomed to wander, without love.

He had always written single songs. 'Adelaide' was a popular hit before he was thirty; he had given Josephine 'To Hope', and Antonie 'To the Beloved'. But in April 1816, as if a distant love was that much more inspiring, he wrote *An die ferne Geliebte, To the Distant Beloved*: a whole song-cycle, the first in Western music.

He called it a 'song-ring', *Liederkreis*. The songs run into each other like thoughts. The theme of the first reappears as the end of the last, closing the ring, *Kreis*, a token of love. The lyrics interweave the nature he loved with the image of unattainable love: the singer imagines the wind wafting his songs through woods and valleys to his beloved. When she sings these songs, they will join two loving hearts: separation will be overcome.

What was really overcome was creative aridity. Maybe writing this was emotional closure, or maybe his next style, gestating through four years of misery, was simply ready to go. From November 1816, beginning with Piano Sonata Opus 101 (as if he was going back to his teenage self, improvising on the piano), he wrote himself into a new and astonishing creativity.

For much of 1817 he was ill; then he wrote the *Hammerklavier Sonata*. He worried about money: 'I have enough boards for one more window shutter,' he wrote in his diary. 'What do blankets cost?' But he stopped writing a diary, as if he no longer needed it now he was composing.

He gave up trying to hear what people said, and began carrying notebooks for them to write in. His *Conversation Books* also contain shopping lists and necessities: 'Blotting sand. Russian night candles. Coffee cup for housekeeper. Ink. Spices. Pottery shaving mug. Shit shovel. What do people wear now instead of an undershirt?'

These were the domestic minutiae against which his late style – introspective, cosmic, radical – evolved. He was experimenting with fragmentation, new possibilities of variation, and ancient polyphonic textures. 'A new and really poetic element must be introduced into the old traditional forms,' he wrote as he prepared to weld this polyphonic lyricism into the sparer textures of a string quartet.

But his late style evolved in a legal and emotional firestorm. All love focused on Karl. 'I am his true father,' he wrote in his diary. Johanna petitioned the tribunal for guardianship and was rejected, but in December 1818 Karl ran away to her. Beethoven asked police to bring him back and wept as he returned Karl to school. 'He's ashamed of me,' he said.

Johanna petitioned again, saying Karl wanted to get away from Beethoven. The tribunal now interviewed everyone and Beethoven let slip that he and Karl's father were not aristocrats: the Flemish *van* in their name was not, like German *von*, a mark of nobility. This tribunal, set up for aristocratic disputes only, and passed the case to a lower court which transferred guardianship to Johanna and a municipal employee.

Meanwhile, in August 1819, brother Johann bought a big estate west of Vienna and wrote to Beethoven signing himself, 'Your brother Johann, landowner'. Beethoven was now in debt, increasingly ill with rheumatic fever, 'gout in the chest', jaundice and a painful liver, and wore a body belt 'owing to the sensitive condition of my abdomen'. He wrote back to Johann signing himself, 'Your brother Ludwig, brain owner', tried to buy a house himself, and failed.

He kept appealing to the court. Finally, in 1820, when Karl was fourteen, he used a personal testimonial from Archduke Rudolph and got sole custody.

In 1821 he was arrested as a tramp in Baden. 'I am Beethoven!' he said. Of course you are, said the Baden constable and threw him in jail. He made such a fuss the policeman disturbed the commissioner at dinner, Beethoven was recognised, set free and apologised to. One wonders if he remembered arguing his father out of jail.

Meanwhile, four commissions led to his last great works. In 1817, the Philharmonic Society of London asked for two symphonies. He began writing the Ninth Symphony, bringing a choir and soloists into the last movement to sing Schiller's 'Ode to Joy' which he had wanted to set since his teenage years with the Illuminati.

Seven years later, 7 May 1824, he conducted the premiere, his first stage appearance in twelve years. He beat time, stretching to his toes, crouching, waving his arms, while the players followed the real conductor behind. Beethoven did not realise when they finished and went on conducting until the alto soloist gently turned him round to see, since he could not hear, the wild applause.

In 1819, the publisher Diabelli asked for piano variations on a waltz and Beethoven wrote the 'Diabelli' Variations, perhaps his greatest piece for piano.

Also in 1819, Archduke Rudolph asked for a mass to celebrate his enthronement as Archbishop at Olmütz. Beethoven began on the *Missa Solemnis*, but by the time of Rudolph's celebration he had only reached the Credo. 'We heard the master howling and stamping behind closed doors,' said his assistant Anton Schindler. 'The door opened and Beethoven stood facing us with features so distorted as to fill one with alarm. He looked as if he had just survived a life-and-death battle.' Beethoven finished it in 1823 and wrote on the score, 'From the heart – may it go to the heart.'

The fourth commission led to his last quartets. In 1822 Prince
Galitsin, a Russian amateur cellist, asked for a set of three.
I saw the manuscripts of two in Poland, in the Archiwum
Uniwersytet Jagielloński, Kraków.

Beethoven began them in 1824, the year Karl entered Vienna
University to study philology. Karl really wanted to join the
army, but Beethoven was against it; Karl later switched to
Business Studies at the Polytechnic. Obsessing over Karl
and sex, Karl and money, Beethoven asked his friends and
Karl's landlord to spy on him.

Beethoven finished Opus 127 in January 1825, and at once
began sketching another quartet but fell seriously ill. In
May 1825 he recovered, went to Baden and began on
Opus 132. He wrote the slow movement, a 'Holy Song of
Thanks' for his recovery, in the archaic Lydian mode
anciently associated with healing. 'I came with a cold and
catarrh,' he wrote to Karl in June, 'my constitution being
naturally rheumatic which will, I fear, soon cut the thread
of my life. Send your linen here; your grey trousers must
still be wearable; for, my dear son, you are indeed
very dear to me! My address is, "At the coppersmith's." I
embrace you from my heart. Your faithful and true
FATHER.'

But he was tormented by the idea of Karl seeing his mother
behind his back. Other letters he wrote that month,
as he finished Opus 132, reflect the almost nuclear power
he must have had of splitting (as in the 'deep lovely
thoughts' of his *raptus* long ago) his creative imagination
from his feelings about other people. 'Someone tells me

you and your mother have again been associating in secret. Am I to again experience the most horrible ingratitude? God is my witness my sole dream is to get away from you and that horrible family foisted upon me.'

Then he began Opus 130. Distraught to hear that Karl was now living with his mother, he wrote *molto espressivo* above the crisis of that quartet, the Cavatina. One section, where the three lower voices break into dusky triplets and the first violin responds with lonely choked-off cries, he marked *beklemmt*: anguished, stifled.

In October 1825, he moved back to Vienna, to lodgings in the Schwarzspanierhaus, House of the Black Spaniards, near his friend Stephan von Breuning. Stephan's wife helped with housekeeping and maybe he felt some whisper of the care he first experienced when he met Stephan's family in Bonn. He enjoyed the company of Stephan's thirteen-year-old son Gerhardt, whom he nicknamed Trouserbutton.

After fulfilling his commission of three quartets, he went on to write more. In December, he began Opus 131, using, 'A new manner of part-writing, and, thank God, less lack of imagination than before,' he told violinist Karl Holz.

He normally left Vienna in the summer, but in 1826 he stayed to keep an eye on Karl, now nineteen and living in a boarding house. They had arguments over money, Karl's friends, how he spent his time, whether he was working hard enough. During one row Karl hit him, fled to his mother, and told one of the friends Beethoven sent to spy on him that he was going to shoot himself. The landlord removed two pistols he found in Karl's trunk and Beethoven went on with Opus 131.

At the end of July, Karl pawned his watch, bought more pistols, went to Baden where he had often stayed with Beethoven, climbed the castle ruins outside town and fired both guns at his head. The first bullet missed, the second grazed his temple. He was found bleeding and taken to his mother, then to hospital.

Beethoven rushed round Vienna distraught saying, 'My Karl has a bullet in his brain. I love him so much.' But when he was finally allowed into the hospital, he told a doctor, 'Is my scoundrel of a nephew here? I didn't want to visit him, he doesn't deserve it, he has made me too much trouble.' Karl wrote in the *Conversation Book,* 'Don't torment me with reproaches and complaints.' Five days later Beethoven took Opus 131 to the printer.

Stephan urged Beethoven to let Karl join the army. A Lieutenant-Marshal Baron von Stutterheim said he would admit Karl to his regiment, and Beethoven dedicated Opus 131 to him in gratitude.

But Karl's scar had to heal first, and Beethoven's brother Johann invited Beethoven and Karl to stay. Just as Beethoven fled to one brother's house in the siege, now he took refuge in the other's. At the end of September, he and Karl made the two-day journey to Johann's mansion near the village of Gneixendorf. He brought with him the unfinished manuscript of Opus 135.

The countryside reminded him of the Rhineland, and his rooms had murals of the Rhine commissioned by Johann in memory of their childhood, but there was friction all round. Beethoven was jealous of Karl's relations with Therese and her daughter, even though Therese wrote in the *Conversation Book*, 'It is you Karl loves, to the point of veneration.' On 1 December, he and Johann had a row, Johann refused to provide a closed carriage for the trip back, so Beethoven trundled off with Karl on an open cart and returned to Vienna dangerously ill.

Karl looked after him, but on 2 January 1827, Karl went off to the army. Beethoven never saw him again. He grew weaker and weaker. Old friends visited, Trouserbutton kept popping in to cheer him up. He was delighted by £100 from the Philharmonic Society of London, talked of writing another symphony for them and visiting London when he was better, read Walter Scott and Homer, tried finally to learn the multiplication tables, wrote letters, thanked his old landlord Baron Pasqualati for a bottle of champagne.

When he was nearly unconscious, a case of Rhine wine arrived, wine from his homeland. 'Pity, too late,' he said and they gave him a spoonful. In a storm on 26 March there was a flash of lightning, he raised his fist in a muscle spasm or last defiance, and was gone. They performed an autopsy to discover, as he requested, the cause of his deafness. One detail recorded was 'exaggerated folds' of his brain: 'twice as deep as usual and more numerous, more spacious'. On the day of his funeral, Vienna's schools were closed and thousands of people followed the cortège through the streets.

A SELECTION
OF HIS WORKS

Music in the Dark of the Mind

Birth to Twenty-one: 1770–92

1782	*Variations Pour le Clavecin*, WoO 63
1785	Quartets for Piano and Strings, WoO 36
1790	*Cantata on the Death of Emperor Joseph*, WoO 87
1790	*Cantata on the Accession of Leopold II*, WoO 88

Virtuoso

Twenty-one to Thirty-one: 1792–1802

1794–95	Piano Trios, Opus 1
1795	Piano Sonatas, Opus 2
1795	First Piano Concerto, Opus 15
1788–95	Second Piano Concerto, Opus 19
*c.*1795	'Adelaide', Song, Opus 46
1796	Cello Sonatas, Opus 5
*c.*1796	*Duet for Viola and Cello with Two Obbligato Eyeglasses*, WoO 32
1797–98	String Trios, Opus 9
1797	Piano Trio, Opus 11
1796–98	Piano Sonatas, Opus 10

1798	Violin Sonatas, Opus 12
1798	'Pathétique' Piano Sonata, Opus 13
1799–1801	String Quartets, Opus 18
1799–1800	Septet, Opus 20
1795–1801	First Symphony, Opus 21
1801	*Creatures of Prometheus*, Ballet, Opus 43
1801	'Moonlight' Piano Sonata, Opus 27, No. 2
1801–02	Second Symphony, Opus 36
1801–02	Violin Sonatas, Opus 30
1802	'Tempest' Piano Sonata, Opus 31, No. 2
1802	'Eroica' Variations for Piano, Opus 35
1802	*Christ on the Mount of Olives*, Opus 85

Hero

Thirty-two to Forty-one: 1803–12

1803–04	Third Symphony, *Eroica*, Opus 55
1803	'Kreuzer' Violin Sonata, Opus 47
1803–04	*Andante Favori*, WoO 57
1804	'Waldstein' Piano Sonata, Opus 53
1804–06	'Appassionata' Sonata, Opus 57
1805	'To Hope', Song, Opus 32
1804–05	*Fidelio* (first & second versions), Opus 72
1805–06	Fourth Piano Concerto, Opus 58
1806	String Quartets, Opus 59
1806	Fourth Symphony, Opus 60
1806	Violin Concerto, Opus 61
1807	Mass in C major, Opus 86
1804–08	Fifth Symphony, Opus 67
1802–08	Sixth Symphony, *Pastoral*, Opus 68

1808	Cello Sonatas, Opus 69
1808	'Choral Fantasia', Opus 80
1809–11	Fifth Piano Concerto, 'Emperor', Opus 73
1809–10	'Les Adieux' Piano Sonata, Opus 81a
1809	'Harp' String Quartet, Opus 74
1810	'Für Elise', Bagatelle, WoO 59
1809–10	Overture & Incidental Music, *Egmont*, Opus 84
1810	String Quartet, *Quartetto Serioso*, Opus 95
1811	'To the Beloved', Song, WoO 140
1812	Allegretto for Piano Trio, WoO 39
1811–12	Seventh Symphony, Opus 92
1810–11	'Archduke' Piano Trio, Opus 97

You Must Not Be Human

Forty-one to Fifty-six: 1812–27

1812	Eighth Symphony, Opus 93
1812	*Three Equals for Four Trombones*, WoO 30
1812	Violin Sonata, Opus 96
1813	'Battle' Symphony, Opus 91
1816	*To the Distant Beloved*, Song-Cycle, Opus 98
1816	Piano Sonata, Opus 101, No. 28
1818	'Hammerklavier' Sonata, Opus 106
1820	Piano Sonata, Opus 109
1821	Piano Sonata, Opus 110
1821–22	Piano Sonata, Opus 111
1819–23	'Diabelli' Variations, Opus 120
1819–23	*Missa Solemnis*, Opus 123
1822–24	Ninth Symphony, *Choral*, Opus 125
1824–25	String Quartet, Opus 127

1825	String Quartet, Opus 132
1825–26	String Quartet, Opus 130
1826	String Quartet, Opus 131
1825–26	*Grosse Fuge*, Opus 133
1826	String Quartet, Opus 135

FURTHER READING

Albrecht, T., editor and translator, *Beethoven's Conversation Books*, Vol. 1, The Boydell Press, 2018

Breuning, Gerhard von, *Memories of Beethoven: In the House of the Black-Robed Spaniards*, ed. M. Solomon, CUP, 1992

Cooper, Barry, *The Beethoven Compendium*, Thames & Hudson, 1991

—*Beethoven*, OUP, 2008

Eaglefield-Hull, A., *Beethoven's Letters*, translated and edited by J. S. Shedlock, Dover Publications, 1926

Hamburger, Michael, editor and translator, *Beethoven: Letters, Journals, Conversations*, Thames & Hudson, 1951

Lockwood, Lewis, *Beethoven, The Music and the Life*, W. W. Norton & Company, 2003

Solomon, M., *Beethoven*, Schirmer Books, 1977

—*Late Beethoven: Music, Thought, Imagination*, University of California Press, 2003

Sonneck, O. G., editor, *Beethoven, Impressions by his Contemporaries*, G. Schirmer Inc., 1926

Suchet, John, *Beethoven: The Man Revealed*, Elliott & Thompson, 2017

Swafford, Jan, *Beethoven: Anguish and Triumph*, Faber, 2015

Skowroneck, T., *Beethoven the Pianist*, CUP, 2010

Thayer, A. W., *Life of Beethoven*, ed. Elliot Forbes, Princeton University Press, 1970

Tyson, Alan, editor, *Beethoven Studies 3*, CUP, 1982

Watson, Angus, *Beethoven's Chamber Music in Context*, The Boydell Press, 2010

Wegeler, Franz and Ries, Ferdinand, *Beethoven Remembered: Biographical Notes* (1838), translated by F. Bauman and T. Clark (1906), Great Ocean Publishers, 1987

ACKNOWLEDGEMENTS

We know directly about Beethoven's life from five main sources. His sketchbooks are a unique detailed record of his creative process: thousands of pages in which he worked out musical ideas but also scribbled occasional personal thoughts. There are thousands of letters and also two diaries. One is an expenses log, the Memorandum Book he kept when he first came to Vienna, the other a journal he wrote for six years in his forties. Finally, from 1818 on, when completely deaf, he carried home-made *Conversation Books* for people to write in. Most entries in these are by other people but occasionally he writes shopping lists, or copies out ads for flats. Or, if the conversation is in public and he wants no one else to hear, he writes his replies.

In addition, close friends wrote memoirs of him and contemporaries mention him in letters. He was well known, famously eccentric, and loved company, joking, drinking and eating in taverns. He made warm friendships, especially with other musicians, and had a gift for enjoying people as well as exploding at them. So there are hundreds of stories: some conflict with each other, many may not be true. His first biographer, Alexander Wheelock Thayer, interviewed people who knew him but they may not have told the truth or remembered correctly.

From all this, drawing also on police records, coach timetables and hotel registers, biographers and scholars have tried to sift false from true, and piece his life together, sometimes in extraordinary detail. Recent research suggests that some often-told anecdotes and ideas about his life on which a few of my poems are based – such as what Mozart said about him, whether he got on with Haydn, how harsh his father really was, visits to brothels, his drinking before he tried to propose to Therese – may be apocryphal or speculative. But I have tried to make the poems reflect as accurate a historical picture, and open up as many insights which might deepen enjoyment of the music, as I can.

Many people have helped with this book and I am grateful to them all, especially David Waterman who dreamed up concerts with me, lent me books, and talked Beethoven with me for years; and to his colleagues in the Endellion String Quartet, for concerts in which they played music and I read the first versions of these poems. Many thanks also to Paul Barritt and Tring Chamber Music, for commissioning poems, inviting me to read them in concerts, and talk in intervals between Paul's extraordinary performance, over a single weekend, of all the Violin Sonatas. The Aspect Foundation puts on unique chamber music concerts in New York and London which mix music and words. I am deeply grateful to Irina Knaster, who founded and runs it, for talking Beethoven with me and commissioning me to write poems which became the beginning of this book.

The Corporation of Yaddo gave me a wonderful month's writing among snowy trees, deer, wild turkeys and clear moons. It was a privilege to work there and I am grateful to the Corporation and staff, and to comments from other artists there at the time.

For detailed comments on poems I am very grateful to Daphne Astor, Gwen Burnyeat, Jane Duran, David Harsent, Andrei Gomez-Suarez, Alberto Manguel and Declan Ryan.

For further thoughts, and conversations on playing and listening to Beethoven, many warm thanks to Thomas Adès and Steven Isserlis – and a big thank you to Steven for encouraging me to end the poems on a note of hope rather than heartbreak. On Vienna and its complexities, many thanks to Angelika Klammer. Many thanks to everyone at Chatto, especially Parisa Ebrahimi, dedicated editor, and Charlotte Humphery. I am also very grateful to Barry Cooper for correcting and refining historical details.

Further back, many thanks to my family for playing music with me and sharing all that lucky musical growing-up, and my parents for making that happen. Also my viola teacher Kay Hurwitz, and Sheila Nelson who taught violin to my sister, two of my brothers and my daughter, for her inspirational approach to playing, especially chamber music. It was a privilege to watch her teach. I am also warmly grateful to my piano teacher Olive Lewin, especially for encouraging me to sing. I have learned a lot since from her book, *Rock It Come Over*, about her own musical journey, joining a classical concert pianist training to her career in preserving Jamaican folk music.

I also enjoyed singing Cole Porter with Alan Tyson, a Beethoven scholar famous for, among other things, deciphering Beethoven's blotchy handwriting. I remember turning up for coffee one morning when he was working on a manuscript: a memorable picture of someone completely happy in his work. He pioneered work on dating manuscripts by watermarks on paper, and is behind the Stained Manuscripts poem somewhere so thank you, Alan.

*

Thanks to editors of these publications, where some of these poems first appeared:

Echoes of Paradise: On the 350th Anniversary of John Milton's Epic, ed. Edward Allen (Cambridge, Christ's College, 2020); *Financial Times*
New York Review of Books
The Scores: A Journal of Poetry and Prose.